SET FREE

FOREWORD BY JOHN SEIGENTHALER

SET FREE

Discover Forgiveness Amidst Murder and Betrayal

STEPHEN OWENS   KEN ABRAHAM

Nashville, Tennessee

978-1-4336-8023-6

Published by B&H Publishing Group

Nashville, Tennessee

Dewey Decimal Classification: 234.5

Subject Heading: FORGIVENESS \ HOMICIDE \
MOTHER-SON RELATIONSHIP

Unless otherwise noted, Scripture quotations are from the
New International Version, copyright © 1973, 1978, 1984 by
International Bible Society.

Scripture quotations marked (HCSB) are taken from the Holman
Christian Standard Bible® Copyright © 1999, 2000, 2002, 2003,
2009 by Holman Bible Publishers. Used by permission.

1 2 3 4 5 6 7 8 • 17 16 15 14 13

ACKNOWLEDGMENTS

Writing an emotionally charged book such as *Set Free* could have easily imprisoned me once again had it not been for the help and encouragement of so many people. Others, while not actively involved in the process of producing this book, have invested in my life in ways that I can never repay, yet for which I will always be grateful.

At the risk of missing someone, I want to express my heartfelt thanks to:

Gaile Owens—Thank you for taking these steps with me and moving forward. Thank you for believing in our future one day at a time. I admire your courage and strength displayed in the incredible progress you have made during this transition. I am grateful for your support, love, and encouragement as we both walk through healing and reconciliation.

John Seigenthaler—Thank you, John, for embracing Mom's case and for writing the initial articles that moved her story out of the prison and into the newspaper, and for your friendship and fatherly support to me.

Katy Varney—For putting your heart on the line, as well as your time, energy, and the resources of your company; for your support and tireless work on behalf of my mom, I will always be indebted.

Kelley Henry—Thanks for your hard work on Mom's case, and for never giving up!

Gretchen Swift—Thank you for your heartfelt work on Mom's case, but most of all for your sincere friendship with Mom.

Carolyn Hensley—Thank you for having the faith and courage to take in two little boys, raising us as your own, and instilling Christian principles in us. Thank you for your unwavering love.

Ken Abraham—For your hard work on writing this book. And for your compassion to tell it in a way that was respectful but powerful.

Bob Starnes—You believed in this project from the beginning, and your unrelenting perseverance helped turn our hopes and dreams for a book into a tangible reality. Thanks, too, Bob, for your incredible friendship and support.

Trevor Starnes—For your incredible research on the front end of this book to help shape the direction that will impact lives.

Brock Starnes—For your attention to detail with design and marketing and behind the scenes support that added so much to this book. You are truly gifted!

Dawn Woods—Thank you for believing in this project, Dawn, and for your willingness to take a chance on my story.

The entire B&H Publishing Group editorial, marketing, and sales team—thank you for believing in and taking my story to the world.

Drew Maddux—For your great friendship and support as I went through this chapter in my life.

Steve Wilson—Thank you for befriending my mother and ministering to her long before I was ready to be reconciled with her. Thanks, too, for challenging, supporting, and encouraging me to follow what I thought God was calling me to do.

My elementary school teachers: Mrs. Orman, Mrs. Gann, and Mrs. Lawrence—You were there for me during some of my darkest days, and you refused to let me fall through the cracks. Thank you for your continuous support and the significant roles you have played in my life for more than twenty-eight years.

My brother, Brian Owens—We've lived through a nightmare together and have come out stronger. Though we grew up without our dad, we've always had a heavenly Father, and my prayer is that He will continue to guide our steps—together.

My wife Lisa, and sons, Zachary and Joshua—Thank you for loving me throughout this process. To Lisa, especially, thank you for walking with me in the good times and the bad, and never wavering in your love and support for me. God has truly blessed me through you.

Most of all, I give thanks to God who has reconciled us to Himself through Jesus.

CONTENTS

*Then Peter came to Him and said, "Lord, how
many times could my brother sin against me and
I forgive him? As many as seven times?"
"I tell you, not as many as seven," Jesus said to him,
"but 70 times seven."*
—MATTHEW 18:21–22 (HCSB)

FOREWORD

Stephen Owens is my close, relatively newfound friend, a fact, I suppose, that surprises us both since I am old enough to be his grandfather.

Stephen is too young to write an autobiography. But, fortunately for readers of this book, he has decided to relate the story of how the events that shocked and shaped his boyhood, and shadowed his adult life, finally moved him to confront and resolve the emotional inner conflict that always haunted his heart. It is the story of his conflicted spiritual journey. It has relevance for many who have faced adversity, perhaps burdened in reaction with anger, hatred, confusion, frustration, and mistrust.

Imagine Stephen as a lad of ten, eleven, and twelve years of age who sees his life at that interval as near-idyllic: He and his little brother, three years his junior, live with parents who love them in a comfortable suburban home in Bartlett, near Memphis, Tennessee. Ron Owens, his father, is an administrator at a leading community hospital; Gaile, his mother, works as an aide to a medical doctor.

The family, devoutly Christian, attends church faithfully. It is a close-knit congregation of friends, almost an extended family.

On a February Sunday evening, the viewfinder through which twelve-year-old Stephen has seen this happy home life is shattered by a mind-numbing act of criminal violence: His father is brutally murdered.

Five days later comes the searing, sickening understanding of a betrayal that finally destroys the near-perfect world young Stephen thought he knew. His mother is arrested by police and charged with hiring a stranger to kill his father.

Less than a year later, Stephen finds himself in a courtroom testifying against his mother, who is on trial for his father's murder. He tells the jury about discovering his father, his head bloodied and bashed, as he gasped his last breaths. At trial's end, his mother and the stranger she promised money to kill her husband both receive death sentences.

Stephen does not see or speak to his mother again for almost a quarter century.

I was asked by Stephen to write this foreword because he knew I had been part of a small group, mostly lawyers, who came together to try to devise a strategy to save Gaile Owens from the jury's death sentence. Our circle met often, constantly evaluating possible initiatives that might persuade the judicial system to spare her life, or move the governor, who had the power to commute her death sentence.

Initially, I participated in these strategy sessions because I believe that the death penalty is an offense against reason and religion; an affront to the constitutional bar against cruel and unusual punishment; a rejection of the biblical mandate that begins, "thou shalt not . . ." To those of us who oppose capital punishment, elongated incarceration, even life without parole, seems more rational than snuffing out a citizen's life—even one who commits unspeakable crimes.

In fact, it was not necessary to pass a litmus test on capital punishment in order to oppose the state killing of Gaile Owens. To meet and come to know her, even in the uncomfortable visiting quarters of a prison, was to recognize that she was intelligent, articulate, thoughtful, and considerate. She had, over long years behind the walls, earned the respect and affection of her lawyers, the thanks of her prison custodians, whose jobs she sought to make less stressful, and the regard of her sister-inmates, many of whom relied on her for sage advice early in their incarceration.

But now, Gaile Kirksey Owens was about to become the first woman in 189 years to be executed by the state of Tennessee.

The question always for those of us who hoped she would live, was to wonder how such a clear-headed, sensitive, religiously-influenced woman could have been guilty of arranging her husband's murder.

Finally, the state set the date of her execution: September 28, 2010. Now only a commutation by the governor would spare her life.

For years Stephen had, again and again, turned away his mother's lawyers when they had come to him seeking statements of support for her. Stephen had decided long before, that never would he lift a finger or raise his voice to help her. He thought his mother deserved to die. He had never forgiven her.

Now his mother was destined to die and my hope was that his attitude might change.

This is Stephen's story. I must not intrude further. He tells it with refreshing candor and simple eloquence, detailing both the pain and the healing that he experienced. He was helped in the composition and publishing by Ken Abraham, a gifted writer, and by Stephen's friend and adviser, Bob Starnes.

To me, Stephen's story, quite simply, is a parable. Its moral is pregnant with meaning for us all, and particularly those whose lives are clouded by forces of fate beyond their control. Read it for its moral—and its message of love.

John Seigenthaler

PREFACE

B arbed wire.

    I couldn't take my eyes off the barbed razor wire atop the chain link fence surrounding the prison complex, as my wife Lisa and I drove onto the property of the Tennessee Prison for Women.

The red brick administrative building at the front of the prison looked much like a modern day high school—except for the wire—but the benign exterior appearance belied the fact that beyond that welcoming frontage was a maximum security prison. Inside those fences, gates, and walls lived my mother.

My mom, Gaile Kirksey Owens, had been incarcerated in this prison facility since February 21, 1986. It was now August 2009 and I had not seen her face since I had testified against her in court more than twenty-three years earlier and had helped the prosecutors convict her of *parricide*, "accessory before the fact to first-degree murder," for hiring a man to murder my dad. Although Mother had immediately confessed, there was good reason my testimony against her carried such weight, even as a mere twelve-year-old child. On that horrible night a few days after Valentine's Day in 1985, I was the one who had discovered my dad facedown on the floor of our den, his head bludgeoned and bloody, beaten nearly to death with a tire iron, by a man whose horrific crime had originated in the heart and mind of my own mother.

Dad died a few hours later, and Mother and her accomplice were apprehended and indicted the following week. For the next quarter of a century, I had nothing to do with her. I didn't see her, rarely spoke with her, and did not write to her until after Lisa's and my first child was born. For most of that time, although I knew she was in prison, because of my own anger and bitterness toward her, I did not even know my own mother's whereabouts. Nor did I care. Not that she would have been hard to find. Since the day she was sentenced and transferred from jail to prison, Mother had lived on "death row" in the same facility, scheduled to be the first woman executed in Tennessee in more than 189 years.

Now as we approached the prison entrance on this summer day, I could feel the perspiration dotting my forehead even in the air-conditioned car.

What would I say to her? What words does a son first speak to a mother who set the wheels in motion to violently murder his father? Could I even look at her? How would she respond to me?

Forces much greater than my own plans or desires were directing my path to the prison. For more than a year now, I had known this trip was inevitable and unavoidable; it would have to occur; I must visit my mother in prison. I had not wanted to do so, but God had been setting me up through circumstances and situations in my own life, inexorably leading me to that prison. He had spoken to me quite emphatically, "I have you right where you are supposed to be, and you know what you are supposed to do."

How could I ignore or attempt to circumvent such specific instructions? I could put off this confrontation no longer.

CHAPTER 1

Murder in Memphis

I should have known something was up when Mother informed my younger brother Brian and me that we were going to Aunt Carolyn's house to play games after church on Sunday night. Sunday night? "Please, Mom, can't we go with Dad?" I begged.

"Yeah, we want to stay with Dad," Brian echoed. "Please, Mom. Can we?"

Ordinarily, if our family didn't go straight home after evening church services, Brian and I would go with Dad to the gymnasium on the property, where Dad coached the church basketball team. At ages eight and twelve, Brian and I considered Dad as our hero who could do no wrong and we loved being with him any time, especially when he was playing or coaching basketball.

But on that night, Sunday, February 17, 1985, Mother insisted that we go to Aunt Carolyn's house, about two blocks away from the church, to play board games. It just didn't feel right. It was almost as though Mom didn't want us to go home.

We ate a late snack and then played games for several hours, leaving Aunt Carolyn's around 10:30 p.m. Our two-story home in Bartlett, a suburb of Memphis, was located on a corner lot on Sceptor Drive, a peaceful, quiet, residential area lined with large oak trees. Even late at night, it had a safe feeling to it. But when we finally got back to the house shortly before 11:00 p.m., the moment we made the turn and pulled into the driveway, I noticed Dad's Honda Prelude sitting in the driveway with its driver's side door open, the interior light still on. That was odd. Dad's sports jacket and tie were still lying over the back of the car seat, as though he had gone into the house and would be coming back out momentarily. That was unusual, too. Dad was a particular dresser, and he was not one to leave his good sports jacket rumpled in the car.

As soon as Mom pulled her Oldsmobile Cutlass Supreme into the driveway behind Dad's car, I hopped out and shut Dad's car door, just like I knew he would want me to do. I continued around to the back of the house and found the large wrought iron door to our laundry room and kitchen unlocked. The door was ajar and the keys were still in the lock.

I pushed the door open and stepped inside. When I walked into the kitchen, I was shocked. The place was a mess! The chairs to the kitchen table had been overturned and lay sideways on the floor. Dad's yellow Puma gym bag looked as though it had been slung over the kitchen table, with the contents strewn in every direction. Something red—something that looked like blood—was spattered and smeared on the wall and the floor.

A dim lamp was on in the den, so I turned the corner past the laundry room, walked through the kitchen, and naively stepped into the den. The sight I saw will haunt me for the rest of my life.

There, lying face down on the floor, with his head turned away from me, near the fireplace, was my dad. At first, I thought he might be sleeping since Dad sometimes fell asleep on the floor while watching television after an exhausting workout, so I gingerly slipped over to him. I peered down intently at him, shook him slightly, and rolled him over. That's when I saw the blood, which was already soaking the beige carpet in front of the fireplace. I looked more closely at my dad's head and it was obvious that he had been in a fight. His nose looked crooked, his head and face were severely beaten and bloody. It was then that I heard the awful sounds in Dad's throat. Even as a twelve-year-old kid, I knew my hero was dying.

Frozen in place with fear, and not knowing what else to do, I screamed.

Mom rushed to the doorway and when she saw the grotesque scene in the den, she screamed as well. "He's been shot!" she wailed. Instinctively, she drew Brian to her and would not allow him to enter the room. "Stephen, get out of there," she called to me from the doorway. "Come on; we have to get out of here."

Although I was too horror-stricken to think straight at the time, Mom's response later puzzled me. Shot? Why in the world would Mother think that Dad had been shot? There was no evidence of a gun. There were no bullet casings, no shells, and no weapon lying on the floor. *Shot?*

Mom hustled Brian and me out of the den and out the back door to the neighbors' house, where she called the police and an ambulance. Help arrived in a matter of minutes, but the severe trauma Dad had suffered from the multiple blows to his head and face were more than his body could withstand. He remained unconscious and barely breathing as the ambulance roared out of our driveway, the siren blaring on the way to the hospital.

An autopsy later revealed that Dad had been bludgeoned, hit at least twenty-one times in the head by a blunt instrument, thought to be a tire iron. The blows were so severe, they had driven Dad's face into the floor, crushed his skull, and forced bone fragments into his brain.

Apparently, Dad had put up quite a fight. Police investigators later determined that Dad's assailant had been hiding in the storage shed and had attacked him from behind as he opened the door to the house. The attacker somehow forced the altercation inside the house and Dad fought him around a staircase and into the den, but the violent blows from the steel tire tool were overpowering, and Dad went down. That didn't stop his assailant, who the police determined had struck Dad several times in the face and head even when he was already incapacitated, unable to fight back anymore, and lying on the floor. The medical and forensic investigators discovered strands of Dad's own hair between his fingers, and found that Dad had also sustained extensive injuries to his hands, indicating that he had attempted to cover his head as he was being beaten with the tire iron. The madman who had done this horrific deed had been relentless in his attack.

Brian and I remained at the neighbors' home while Mom went on to the hospital to be with Dad, and to answer questions from the police. At about three o'clock in the morning, Brian and I were transferred to our pastor's daughter and son-in-law's residence, as the police combed the area in and around our house looking for clues. When the sun came up, they continued their investigation, eventually conducting a search of Dad's office at the hospital, and interviewing numerous friends, coworkers, and business acquaintances of our family.

My brother and I didn't go to school that next day. We were worried sick about Dad. About mid-morning, Mom and our minister, Pastor Jimmy Greer, gathered Brian and me and other family members to tell us that Dad had not made it. At 2:40 a.m., less than four hours after I had found him on the floor, Dad had passed away. I was overwhelmed with grief. My dad, my mentor, my best friend, and my hero was dead.

The next few days spun by in a blur as we prepared for Dad's funeral. Mom seemed deeply troubled, sullen and sad, which seemed normal to everyone, especially me. Who wouldn't be upset if a family member had been murdered—and for no apparent reason? Nothing seemed to be missing from our home, so obviously the assailant's motive had not been burglary. Why would anyone want to hurt our dad? And if Dad was targeted, was anyone else in our family or neighborhood safe?

I didn't notice anything unusual about Mom's demeanor or her actions that week. Although I didn't step into the den, I saw the carpet in the room had been torn up, leaving nothing but an exposed concrete slab. We quickly exited the house and I don't ever remember returning to it. We were all grief-stricken and devastated, being comforted by church folks who wanted to protect us at all costs. It never even crossed my mind that Mother might be involved in Dad's death.

On Friday of that same week, I went to a friend's house, where I was supposed to spend the night with him. But shortly after I arrived, some relatives came and spoke in quiet tones to my friend's mom. I would not be able to spend the night. Instead, they took me to Aunt Carolyn's home.

As soon as I walked in the door, I could tell something serious was going on. Aunt Carolyn and Pastor Greer sat Brian and me down and as tactfully as possible told us, "Your mother has been arrested." They tried gently to tell me why Mother had been apprehended, that she had been involved somehow in the murder of my father.

"No!" I cried out. This could not be happening. Somebody has made an awful mistake. Mother loves Dad!

The horrific nightmare was getting worse.

CHAPTER 2

Anything But a Dream

Prior to Dad's death, by all external appearances, our family was reminiscent of the Ward and June Cleaver family of 1960s *Leave It to Beaver* television fame. We weren't a wealthy family, but we enjoyed a comfortable lifestyle and lived in a quiet, residential section of Memphis. I never felt deprived. From all external appearances, we were a happy, conservative Christian family, with healthy relationships.

Dad worked as the Associate Director of Nursing for Baptist Memorial Hospital, an administrative type of job at the downtown hospital. He wore a suit and tie to work every day. Dad was not a doctor, but he had served as a medic during the Vietnam War, and—as I had always been told—was shot at least twice in the line of duty. He had worked as a nurse at LeBonheur Children's Clinic in Memphis, so he had an interest in medicine and an understanding of the medical community, long before he took the job at Baptist.

For most of my early life, Mother had a job outside the home, as well, working as an assistant in the doctor's surgical center. She had a soft, Southern elegance about her, demure and unassuming, quick to smile, and pretty even without makeup, which she used sparingly. Mom loved Dad and she certainly loved her boys—Brian and me. She rarely hesitated to buy us almost anything we asked for when we were with her in a store. Dad, on the other hand, was not inclined to do that. He was much more frugal. He wasn't a spendthrift and he rarely flashed money around or spent lavishly on things we didn't really need.

Dad loved his family and was known around town as a good man and a fine father. By all reports, he had an engaging personality, was smart, charismatic, and had a quick sense of humor. He belonged to a golf club known as Woodstock Hills Country Club. I enjoyed going with Dad to the golf course. Sometimes he let me tee up with him, but even if I didn't play, he allowed me to drive the golf cart, no small thrill for an eight-year-old kid. There was a swimming pool at the club, so sometimes while Dad played golf, Brian, Mother, and I might go to the pool.

We enjoyed family vacations to Tennessee state parks, frequent visits to our grandparents' home in Arkansas, and we took an occasional excursion to Gatlinburg, Tennessee. Sports, vacations, and church were the staples of our lives—especially church.

Life in the Owens home revolved around Abundant Life Fellowship Church, an interdenominational congregation in Memphis. Our family attended services not merely on Sunday morning, but Sunday nights and Wednesday evenings, as well. Mom sang in the church choir, and Dad coached the church basketball team and helped with the softball team, too; so much of our lives centered around church activities. Everyone in the Owens home had made "a profession of faith," declaring himself or herself as a Christian. God was honored in our family. We prayed before nearly every evening meal, and believed the Bible from cover to cover.

Our pastor, Reverend Jimmy Greer, and his wife and children were like extended family members to my family and me. We spent a great deal of time together socially. We celebrated Christmas together, exchanging gifts, and shared close friendships that went beyond the usual pastor-parishioner type relationships. My Aunt Carolyn actually lived with the Greers and their daughters for a while in her late teens and early twenties.

As a boy, I played on the church basketball team, and I was in the Royal Rangers program, similar to the Boy Scouts. I participated in several church drama productions and musicals, as would my brother as he got older. Later, Brian and I attended a Christian school. Our family was thoroughly involved; we were not merely religious folks or fickle Christmas and Easter churchgoers. Our lives were *immersed* in our Christian fellowship.

Abundant Life Fellowship Church was conservative and strict, but not legalistic as some congregations in our denomination were known to be, fussing about hair and clothing styles, jewelry, and other nonessential peccadilloes they associated with conservatism. Instead, our congregation was an enthusiastic group of about three hundred people, and upbeat for the most part; our church teaching was thoroughly orthodox in theology, with a Pentecostal flair.

Reverend Jimmy Greer, Brother Greer, as the congregation affectionately but respectfully referred to him, possessed a strong, booming voice that projected across the congregation commanding attention even without a microphone. As a child I sometimes wondered why Brother Greer was yelling in church, but as I grew older, I came to appreciate his passionate approach to preaching. With dark brown hair and intense eyes, Brother Greer presented a formidable figure standing at the front of the church, especially during seasons of the year when he sometimes grew a beard and mustache. He didn't smile a lot, or if he did, I didn't see him. As much as I loved Brother Greer, I felt intimidated by him during my younger years, but I never doubted his love for the Lord or his commitment to do the right thing, regardless of the cost. He was a pastor who commanded respect and most people in our congregation willingly complied.

Although Mom and Dad were considered dedicated Christians, both held secrets that the congregation as well as the outside world would never have imagined. Nobody outside the family knew, for example, that Mom had experienced a troubled childhood. Years later she claimed to having been emotionally, physically, and sexually abused as a child growing up in a dysfunctional family. "Just keep everyone happy," was Mom's creed. Maintain appearances; bolster the façade that we are the quintessential Christian family, with nary a concern or problem as we travel the road to heaven. Image mattered to Mother, maybe more than anything else. She fostered the notion that "everything was fine" within our family and was quick to guard that perception.

That wouldn't have been so bad, I suppose, but Mom and Dad had much more serious issues.

CHAPTER 3

Behind Closed Doors

Although I knew nothing about it, at the time she was arrested, Mom claimed that she had been living in an emotionally, physically, and sexually abusive relationship from the time she and Dad married. I cannot confirm that Dad ever physically and sexually abused Mom, but I can attest that Mom was psychologically codependent on Dad. She wanted to have a "perfect family" and by outward appearances, she did. No doubt, Mom's futile quest for perfection began many years earlier. Marcia Gaile Kirksey was twenty years old when she moved out of her parents' home and into her own apartment. She went to work for LeBonheur Children's Medical Center in Memphis, where she met Ron Owens, an attractive, physically fit man who would become her husband and Brian's and my father. She adored him immediately. They married in October 1971, and I was born on January 4, 1973. Brian came along three and a half years later.

To help supplement their income, Mom worked as an assistant in a doctor's office. It was while working there that she first used drug samples to help control her weight, as well as some anti-depressants to keep her spirits up, and amphetamines to help improve her energy levels. A naturally pretty, petite woman with a nice figure when she and Dad got married, after the wedding and especially after having a baby, Mom put on about seventy pounds. She suffered from deep insecurities, feeling that she was unattractive, and never able to live up to Dad's expectations. As the Associate Director of Nursing, Dad was constantly surrounded by attractive women, and Mom worried about the potential competition.

Dad fretted over the finances, so in a naïve and foolish attempt to ease the financial stress in their marriage, Mom periodically rifled some funds from the doctor's office. When the physician caught her stealing, Mom promised to repay every penny, which she did—by borrowing money from her mother. Mom repaid the doctor but she was still in debt, so she struck a deal with Grandmother Kirksey by which she could pay her back by doing housecleaning and babysitting chores for her "day care" business, which our grandmother operated out of her own home.

Dad, too, was willing to compromise the truth when it was convenient. He completed his "associates" degree in 1974, but on his job application, he had falsely claimed that he had already earned a bachelors degree. He got the job, but when the hospital discovered his dishonesty, he was placed on probation. More tension developed between Dad and Mom but she was intent on keeping up appearances that everything was fine within our family.

My brother Brian was born in 1976, after which Mom found a new job with another group of doctors. Hoping to please Dad by getting her weight back down as soon as possible, Mom resumed using diet pills; to help relieve her depression she turned to Valium. Because of Dad's inattentiveness to her needs, and the fact that he worked long hours at the hospital, often at night, Mom suspected that Dad was having a sexual affair. She said nothing, but blamed herself for driving him away because of her appearance and their financial stress.

In another misguided effort to win back Dad's affection and approval, Mom turned again to stealing to add to the family income. Over a period of ten months, she forged her employer's name on checks to herself and spent the money on Dad, Brian, me, and others close to her, all in an effort to please people. Once the doctors found out that Mom had stolen from them, they pressed charges against her.

Dad was furious and refused to help her dig out of this mess. Pastor Greer helped arrange for a lawyer to defend Mom and professional psychological counseling with Dr. Max West, to whom Mom went for one session.

Mother pleaded guilty to eight counts of forgery, admitting that she had pilfered money from the local doctors for whom she worked. The District Attorney had agreed that in exchange for her guilty plea, Mother should be sentenced to "time served" and just be required to repay the money and serve five years on probation.

Dad insisted that Mom work to pay back the money she had stolen. He took a better position as the Associate Director of Nursing at Baptist Memorial Hospital, and Mom enrolled in classes at Shelby State Community College, hoping to improve her earning potential. She also got another job as a receptionist—right across the street from Baptist Memorial where Dad worked.

Meanwhile, Dad lived behind a façade of the truth, as well. As Mom and Dad's marriage teetered on the precipice of destruction, Dad found a fatal attraction at the hospital. He had a secret extramarital affair with a hospital coworker. They exchanged letters laced with sexual innuendo, some of which Dad left lying in his desk drawer.

Clearly, deception was rampant in my parents' lives long before it became apparent to others, and Mom and Dad were especially good at hiding it from me. I knew nothing of their struggles until I read about them in court documents twenty-some years later.

CHAPTER 4

I Can't Take It Anymore

W hat would drive a soft-spoken, always smiling Christian woman to hire a hit man to kill her husband? That is a question that has baffled nearly everyone who has investigated my dad's murder.

Though you wouldn't have known it by appearances, Mom was unhappy and depressed; Dad was frustrated and worried about our financial picture.

Possibly, in trying to please Dad, Mother may have lost herself. In the years to come, unseemly information would be revealed about everything from their sex lives to their financial records. Mom contended years later, that from the beginning of their marriage, Dad was sexually abusive and selfish, made fun of her physical appearance, and sexual intimacy was difficult. But there is no proof of any of that other than Mom's word against Dad's, and he was no longer able to speak for himself. Neither are there any police reports, frantic calls for help, photos—nothing that would corroborate Mom's story of an abusive relationship.

Only once did Mother even hint to me that there may be trouble in paradise. "Stephen, if your dad and I were to split up," she asked, seemingly out of the blue, "who would you want to live with?"

I couldn't even fathom such a thing, but I gave her my honest answer. "Dad!"

Whether Mom ever asked Dad for a divorce, I cannot say. I never even heard them have a violent argument, much less talk about dissolving their marriage. Regardless, Mom was convinced that because of her past history of forgery, Dad could easily rip Brian and me out of her life. "You'll never get the boys," was a threat that haunted her, whether real or imagined.

Oddly, even though Dad knew Mom's history of poor money management, he allowed her to handle the household checkbook. Mom continued to spend money we didn't have, repeatedly bouncing checks. Despite Dad's good job and earning good money, the financial stress mounted. The bills kept rolling in and there always seemed to be "too much month at the end of the money." Worse yet, some bills weren't getting paid, and delinquent notices followed closely behind. Mom worried that if Dad found out what was going on, he would divorce her and take Brian and me with him.

Rational or not, Mom's desperation led her to cruise some of the roughest sections of Memphis in search of someone she could hire who would be willing to kill her husband. Driving her blue, relatively new Oldsmobile Cutlass Supreme through Bearwater, a once prosperous industrial section of north Memphis, but by then an area where drug dealers and thugs operated with little fear, Mother was conspicuous. Most people who saw her probably assumed she was looking for a drug deal.

She was. But she wasn't searching for a momentary cocaine high. She was looking for someone who offered a permanent solution to her problems. Maybe she might even be able to cash in on Dad's life insurance policies. With double indemnity payments totaling more than one hundred thousand dollars, she could pay off the bills and make a fresh start. It must have seemed so logical to her at the time.

Over a period of a few months, Mom offered differing amounts of money to various men, attempting to hire someone to kill our dad. One of the men with whom she was negotiating was George Sykes, a convicted murderer; another was George James, who sometimes made a little extra money as a police informant in the seedy sections of Memphis. James played a cat-and-mouse game with Mom, offering to kill dad, and taking some of her money, but never following through. Mother naively shelled out more than four thousand dollars to thugs, with no recourse whenever they reneged on their promises or found some convenient reason to say they couldn't yet get the job done. They played her for a sucker, milking her for money, but Mother was determined. She continued her search.

Looking for James and his cohorts one day, Mother met another man, Sidney Porterfield, a short, strong, fire hydrant of a man, who worked sometimes as a part-time mechanic. Like many men on the streets of Bearwater those days, Porterfield had a record—convicted of robbery with a deadly weapon in 1968 and of simple robbery twice in 1971. Mother supposedly offered him a whopping $17,000 to kill Dad. Porterfield said he wanted to "look into the circumstances."

Mom met with him on at least three occasions, the last being at 2:30 p.m. on that Sunday, February 17, 1985. We had gone to church as a family that morning, and then Dad went out and played golf with one of his friends. Mother, Aunt Carolyn, and

Brian and I had lunch together, before going home for what was supposed to be a relaxing afternoon.

Shortly after lunch, Mother left us, and although we didn't know it at the time, she drove to Raleigh-Frayser to meet Sidney Porterfield. Supposedly, she told him that afternoon that she didn't have the money she'd offered, and couldn't get it until the following week. But she asked Porterfield to go by the house and scope it out, "to get the lay of the land." Porterfield said that he might do so later that day. Mother told him that Dad would either be home alone that night, or would be at the church playing basketball until eight or nine o'clock. She hurriedly drove back home, rounding up Brian and me in plenty of time to make it to the church for the Sunday evening service.

Dad was a little late for church that evening, but he met us there. When he arrived home after playing basketball—while Mom, Brian, and I were still at Aunt Carolyn's—Sidney Porterfield was hiding in the storage room, waiting for Dad.

CHAPTER 5

Caught

Within days of Dad's murder, George James, one of the men Mom had unsuccessfully solicited to kill Dad, contacted the police and told them that Mom had offered him money to do the deed. Ostensibly, James feared that because he had taken money from Mother, he might be a suspect in the murder. Noble fellow that he was, he went to authorities to report the fact that she had been cruising Bearwater wanting to hire someone willing to kill her husband. He agreed to call Mother and allow the police to tap into his phone. With the police listening in, James called Mom, threatening that he would turn her in if she didn't give him more money.

The fact was, before he ever went to the police, George James had already contacted Mother blackmailing her for more money. Mother told him that she didn't have access to any money right now; indeed, because of the crime, all her accounts were frozen and the insurance company would probably take their time making good on the policies she and Dad owned. James, however, was insistent. When Mother told him adamantly that she could not get him any money right now, he decided to get what he could from another source. Or maybe he was just trying to protect himself.

For reasons known only to him, James then assisted the police by permitting them to record additional telephone conversations with Mom, again asking her for "hush money."

Maybe the authorities already had Mother in mind as a suspect. Although it never crossed my mind that Mother could be involved in Dad's death, detectives in any murder case consider the spouse as a prime suspect, due to the sad condition of many modern marriages. Even more disconcerting to Bartlett detective, K. D. Wray, the lead officer on the case, investigators found no physical evidence in the house that might point them to the killer. Not a fingerprint anywhere. Nor could they find a murder weapon.

By dawn on Monday morning, within hours after the murder, the detectives were at Baptist Hospital going through Dad's office looking for clues. When they opened Dad's desk drawer, they found the cards and letters containing salacious content exchanged between my dad and a nurse at the hospital. The police confiscated the letters, and went searching for the nurse.

She wasn't hard to find. When Wray confronted her about her relationship with my father, she confessed willingly. She admitted that they had been having a sexual affair, but said that it had ended some time ago. She also indicated that she knew our family had been struggling financially, largely because of Mother. The woman didn't know anyone who didn't like my dad, and she could not imagine why anyone would want to kill him.

Working together in a makeshift sting operation, downtown Memphis police and Bartlett's Detective Wray tapped George James's phone and listened in as he called Mother. How he knew where to find her is a curious enigma since we had moved out of our house and in with Aunt Carolyn and Uncle Joey during the police investigation. Perhaps the police helped him track down Mother, or possibly someone else gave him the number he needed to reach her. Regardless, when James got Mother on the phone, he pressed her for $1,000 in blackmail money, or else.

Mother reiterated that she couldn't get that much money any time soon. "Give me some time to get the insurance money," she told him, as the detectives recorded her words. "Since he died the way he did, the accounts are frozen."

James pushed Mother for some token money and demanded a face-to-face meeting. She told him she was too busy with family in town for the funeral, but James wouldn't take no for an answer. Exasperated, Mother relented and agreed to meet George James in the parking lot of the JCPenney store at the Raleigh Springs Mall in Memphis. The police heard every word.

Shortly before 3:00 p.m. on Wednesday, February 20, 1985, Mother's blue Cutlass Supreme pulled into the parking lot where George James was pacing nervously. James saw her, and when Mom went into a store—apparently to get some money—he tailed closely behind her. When she came back out of the store, she and James both got into her car, where she gave him two twenty dollar bills and two tens, begging him to keep quiet, telling him that it was all the money she could get.

James was glad to take her cash, but he wanted much more than that. He was, after all, "wearing a wire" installed by Detective Wray and the Memphis detectives, who sat watching and listening in their car parked across the street near Vickers Gas Station. James knew the deal. If this was going to work, he needed Mother's words to be heard. He asked Mom who did the deed.

Mom said that she didn't know.

In a clumsy attempt to get Mom to confess during the recorded conversation, James tried to nudge her into saying something incriminating by asking why she wanted Dad dead anyhow.

"We just had a bad thirteen years," she told her blackmailer. "You don't need to know anything else. Give me a break, okay?"

Mother's next words—all recorded and clearly heard by the detectives—opened up some interesting possibilities. "I've been through a lot. I don't know what's going on, or who did it, or anything. I'm just sitting on pins and needles, and I don't know who else is going to call."

What did Mother mean? Did she really believe that Porterfield had backed off the deal when she couldn't get the money, that she really wasn't aware of his being at the house waiting to murder our dad? Was she expecting other thugs to call, claiming credit for the murder and hoping to get cash out of her?

The most damning element of her statement, however, was that it definitely implied that she knew about the murderer and had, in fact, set the wheels in motion that led to Dad's death.

That's all the detectives needed to hear. They steered straight for Mother's car and surrounded the vehicle.

"What's going on?" Mom said as much to herself as to James.

The detectives informed Mother that she was under arrest for her part in the murder of my father.

When the police played the taped conversation between Mom and James, she immediately confessed her involvement in the murder. "I'm sorry," she said through her tears. "I really don't know, except that I felt like I had had all I could take over the years . . . just the mental abuse I felt I had been through."

Although Mom never denied her guilt, she hedged at first, claiming that she had hired people only to follow Dad and "to rough him up." She admitted paying out between $4,000 to $5,000 to various men she naively thought would do what she asked. Later she confessed to offering three men $5,000 to $10,000 to kill her husband. She also acknowledged talking with a man known to her as "Little Johnny" at 2:30 p.m. on the day of the murder. The topic of discussion? Killing her husband. Although she had promised to pay the killer three or four days after the murder, she hadn't paid him a dime.

The man who met Mom on Sunday afternoon was identified by witnesses as Sidney Porterfield. The police located and arrested him for the murder that same day they arrested my mom. A witness also placed Mr. Porterfield in the vicinity of our home a week before the killing.

Porterfield made a statement to the police that was entered into evidence, confirming Mother's involvement. Porterfield told police he had met with Mom on three occasions to discuss plans for the murder, and that Mom had offered him $5,000 to kill her husband.

When police discovered that shortly after Dad's funeral, Mom had asked our grandfather to borrow $7,000 "to pay some bills," they connected the dots and were convinced she had planned to pay Porterfield with the money. But even the police had to admit no money ever exchanged hands between Mother and Mr. Porterfield.

With no hard evidence, no prints, and not even a murder weapon, in truth, the police case against Porterfield would have been extremely weak, barring two sources of information—his own confession and Mother's confession.

When the police asked why she wanted Dad dead, Mom stated quietly, "We've just had a bad marriage over the years, and I just felt like he had . . . mentally, I just felt like he had been cruel to me." She then made a statement that would create a conundrum.

Minimizing the abuse in Dad's and her marriage that would later be discussed by lawyers, judges, psychologists, and talk-show hosts for years, Mom said simply, "There was very little physical violence." Many would later ask the question how a woman could claim to be physically, emotionally, and sexually abused when "there was very little physical violence."

CHAPTER 6

Trial and Error

Mother was taken to the Bartlett Jail and placed behind bars until her preliminary hearing, after which she would be transferred to the Shelby County Jail in east Memphis a few days later. Because Mother had no money to speak of, and no access to a wide selection of attorneys, Freeman Marr, the Bartlett City Judge, asked Stephen B. Shankman, an attorney in private practice, to meet with Mom in advance of her arraignment and preliminary hearing. In her first meeting with Attorney Shankman, Mom admitted her guilt in attempting to hire Mr. Porterfield to commit the murder, and told the attorney that she did not want to stand trial because she did not want Brian and me to know all the sordid details that led up to what had happened. Nor did she want to sully Dad's name any further. She stressed to the attorney that she wanted to protect Brian and me—no matter what.

Mr. Shankman later recalled in an affidavit, "I met with Ms. Owens the following day and spoke with her for several hours before her arraignment. Ms. Owens was extraordinarily remorseful for hiring someone to kill her husband. But her most immediate and profound concern was the well-being of her children. Ms. Owens was clear—she wanted to plead guilty and avoid a trial because she didn't want to put her children and the rest of her family through any more pain."[1]

In that first meeting, Mother also told the attorney about abuse and the strain in her and Dad's relationship. As Mr. Shankman later noted, "Ms. Owens was also immediately forthcoming with me regarding her motivations for hiring someone to kill her husband—her husband was abusive and cheated on her regularly. Based on the information she provided, I immediately recognized that the defense in this case should be that Ms. Owens suffered from battered women's syndrome."[2]

Stephen Shankman seemed to have a genuine concern for Mom. Unfortunately, she had no money to pay him, so he declined the appointment, and in May 1985 the Shelby County Criminal Court appointed two lawyers, Wayne Emmons and Jim Marty, to represent her. Mother had never before met either of the men, but they were now charged with saving her life.

Mom was quick to tell her new attorneys about Dad's alleged abuse and adultery, and they just as quickly picked up on the battered-wife line of defense. But when the two court appointed attorneys with no budget and very limited staff, asked for money from the court to hire an expert mental health professional to assist with their claim that Mother had endured spousal abuse, Judge Joseph McCartie denied the request. Despite Mr. Marty's lurid and graphic descriptions of what Mom said Dad did to her or had her do to him, the judge was unmoved.

Mr. Emmons admitted his own professional inexperience in the area of battered woman's syndrome. "I've never encountered this before," he said. "I don't know if battered wife syndrome can cause a person to be under the . . . to have a mental disease or defect to the extent that you cannot appreciate the wrongfulness."

Judge McCartie sardonically replied. "Isn't that a question for you to school yourself on as counsel? School yourself," the judge told him. "Either get into the books or talk to psychiatrists."[3]

The judge picked up on one aspect of the Emmons statement—Mother's mental competency to stand trial. He denied money for an expert mental health professional and instead ordered that Mom receive a competency-insanity evaluation from Midtown Mental Health Center in Memphis.

Attorney Emmons protested that they needed more specialized help. "We don't believe that a thirty minute visit by a jail doctor can determine if she needs to be examined psychiatrically for matters that are way beyond the purview of competence to stand trial and insanity at the time of the commission of the alleged offense. We're talking in terms of state of mind. We're talking in terms of criminal intent. We're talking in terms of a highly specialized and very unusual defense, that being battered wife syndrome."[4]

Judge McCartie held his position. The judge was interested in determining only those two issues: Was Mother competent to stand trial, and was she sane or insane at the time she commissioned the murder. Consequently, Mother's attorneys did not receive the expert help and advice they sought, but on October 22, 1985, she was evaluated by Dr. Lynne Zager of Midtown Mental Health Center, with offices located in the Shelby County Jail. Nor did Dr. Zager receive any instructions to determine whether Mother might have experienced abuse in her marriage.

Nevertheless, during Dr. Zager's evaluation of Mother, the matter came up. In her notes of the session, Dr. Zager wrote that Mother had revealed to her "significant information about her relationship with her husband, including affairs, sexual humiliation and over all mistreatment of her, along with the impact his behavior had on her psychologically. Ms. Owens indicated she was depressed, insecure, fearful of him, and could not cope. Ms. Owens was fearful because her husband told her that if she asked for a divorce, he would take custody of the children and keep them from her."[5]

In her notes, the doctor recorded that she did not probe Mom for information about the crime itself because Mother wanted to talk with her attorneys before discussing that with anyone. She was not trying to be uncooperative, in Dr. Zager's estimation.[6] Although considered harmless at the time, Mother's unwillingness to talk about the crime with Dr. Zager proved important, as attorneys and judges later interpreted her restrain as being stubborn and not willing to cooperate with her own defense attorneys.

Ironically, Mom's attorneys did not talk to Dr. Zager about her evaluation of their client, nor did they ask for her files or notes, all of which could have been used in her defense.

In another early conversation that later proved important, Mom told her lawyers about her suspicions that Dad was cheating on her. This too was brought out in the pre-trial hearing, before any jurors were involved. Her lawyers requested from the prosecutor's office any and all information or evidence regarding these matters.

In what would turn out to be a pivotal point, during the pre-trial hearing, the Shelby County District Attorney, Donald Strother, declared, "We have shown them every single scintilla of evidence which we have seized and which we have that came from the house . . . and everything we have in the way of any kind of piece of physical evidence, any piece of paper, any notebook, any-anything along those lines, etcetera that we have, we have made available to them." As emphatic as the DA's inflated, sweeping statement was, it wasn't true.

There were those cards and letters found in Dad's desk at work. They were never turned over to the defense attorneys because Strother allowed them to be returned to the woman with whom Dad had been involved. Detective Wray had interviewed the woman and she had admitted the affair. But because Mother's attorneys were not given the letters, they couldn't prove Dad's actions. Nor did they call the woman to testify, because Mom told her attorneys she didn't want them to drag Dad's name through the mud any more than she already had.

The discussion in court sounded like a "good old boys" version of "Who's On First?"

THE COURT: "Mr. Emmons, who made—who allegedly made the search at the personal property at the office?"

MR. EMMONS: "Your Honor, I'm not sure. I'm not sure if it was police officers or if it was simply hospital personnel cleaning out his—or if it were in fact relatives of the family.

"I believe probably—and this is just a guess based on what information I have—that it was maybe hospital personnel and relatives of the family, and thus, would not involve police officers, but I don't know that for a fact.

"Now, the point I want to stress to the court is that assuming the State exercised a search warrant and seized only certain items, we have no doubt but they would furnish us with everything they seized. But there was a houseful of stuff there. There was an office full of stuff that is not in our possession that is in somebody's possession."

THE COURT: "You claim they're in the State's possession?"

MR. EMMONS: "I claim they could be. I claim that the State has the power and the authority to get those items that we don't have the power and the authority to get. And if we have—in other words, we have got a situation where names, addresses, letters, notes, all sorts of things we believe to be that relate to the extramarital affairs of the deceased and the strange sexual proclivities are in the possession of somebody, and we have. . . ."

THE COURT: "Well, unless they're in the possession of the State, the court has no jurisdiction to order somebody to turn them over."

MR. EMMONS: "I understand that, but I believe the State has the power to reach those items."

THE COURT: "Court is not going to order . . . something such as that. If they don't have them, the court is not going to order them to go out and get them. You have the same authority."

MR. EMMONS: "I don't believe so, Your Honor. I believe Mr. Strother. . . ."

THE COURT: "Well, what power to get a search that you don't have that the State has?"

MR. EMMONS: "Well, I'll just put it this way, Judge, and I've been prosecutor for six or seven years, as the court knows, and defense lawyer for that long, and if as a defense lawyer today, I go pick up a phone and call the administrator of the Baptist hospital or the family and say, 'Look, we'd like all that stuff that came out of the office, they're going to say, "Ha, ha," or whatever they might say.

"If Mr. Strother calls them, they're going to listen to them. He's the prosecutor, he's the district attorney—assistant district attorney. He has the inherent power—he's the prosecutor of this case. He has inherent power to gather and collect evidence . . . I'm saying you're talking about a death penalty case where we're appointed counsel working under time restraints. We've got information out here that we need in order to properly prepare this case and go to the mental. . . ."

THE COURT: "What prevents you to go out and talk to witnesses now?"

MR. EMMONS: "Well, nothing to prevent us from talking to witnesses, but to get these physical items of evidence that we think can be important, there would be. . . ."

THE COURT: "Well, don't you think, number one that you ought to verify whether or not they exist?"

MR. EMMONS: "Oh, yes, sir.

THE COURT: "Well, I would suggest that you do that."

MR. EMMONS: "Well, I would think, too, that. . . ."

THE COURT: "I'm not going to order the State to go do it for you."

MR. EMMONS: "Well, we would ask this . . . Mr. Marty's reminded me of this . . . that if the district attorney has in his possession any of these items that came from the search of the house or the inventory or . . . not search of the office but the inventory of his office, then we feel like under this authority we have a right to that now."

THE COURT: "Do you have an inventory of the office, Mr. Strother?"

MR. STROTHER: "Not that I am aware of, Your Honor."

The District Attorney then reiterated that his office had turned over "every piece of physical evidence" to the defense.

"Well, I certainly accept that," said Emmons. "I've got no reason not to."[7]

No reason not to?

The exchange would have been hilariously funny had they not been talking about evidence that might keep my mother from the electric chair. In addition to the "Bad News Bears" approach by her attorneys, with her insistence on protecting Brian and me, Mother was setting herself up for disaster.

Because Mother's attorneys accepted the District Attorney's word that the prosecution did not have the evidence of Dad's affairs—which they didn't, because the materials had been returned—they gave up on that line of the investigation, just as they had abandoned the battered woman's syndrome information when the judge denied them money to hire an expert.

All of this occurred in the pre-trial hearing. As a result, in February 1986, when Mother stood trial, the jury never heard a word about what Mom may have experienced in her marriage; nor did the jury hear about Dad's unfaithfulness. Instead, the prosecution painted a vivid image of a vicious woman who hired a thug to kill her husband so she could get the insurance money.

Perhaps, the most significant development in Mother's pre-trial events took place right before the trial was to begin, when, with the approval of Dad's family, the prosecutor offered both Mom and Sidney Porterfield a plea bargain. If they would plead guilty, they would receive life sentences, and they would not have to go to trial. With a few signatures, they would be off to prison, and the whole ugly matter could be laid to rest without a public spectacle. The deal was contingent, however, on both Mother and Porterfield accepting the offer.

Except for those first attempts at hedging when she was arrested, Mother had immediately admitted her guilt, was deeply remorseful, and had taken responsibility for her part in the crime. She told her attorney on the day of her arrest that she wanted to plead guilty to protect her boys. So when her attorneys presented the plea bargain from District Attorney Strother just before trial, she signed it without hesitation.

Mr. Porterfield balked. Perhaps his lawyers realized that the police did not really have strong evidence against him other than his confession. Whatever the reason, he had now changed his tune. He claimed that he was not guilty, and wanted to stand trial.

When Porterfield refused to accept the deal, Strother pulled the deal off the table completely for Mom too and withdrew his offer of life in prison. Moreover, the judge refused to separate the two cases. Mother and the murderer would be tried together, at the same time, in the same courtroom and by the same jury. Although Mother had already signed Strother's plea-agreement document, Porterfield would plead not guilty and go to trial. Consequently, because Porterfield was unwilling to admit his guilt, Mother now had to go on trial for her life—for a crime to which she had already agreed to plead guilty, with the death penalty hanging over her head, and the electric chair looming before her.

CHAPTER 7

Inside Information

D espite my young age, because I was the one who first found Dad on the floor of our home, the prosecutors requested that I do a deposition. I really had little information to offer them. I had never seen or heard anything improper between my parents. As far as I knew, we truly were the quintessential family. Oh, sure, occasionally, I heard Mother and Dad arguing over something—usually, the issue was money—but the arguments were never heated or violent. I never witnessed Mother berating my father. I never saw my father strike my mother, or even come close to it. Nor did I hear him emotionally abuse my mother by cursing at her or belittling her in front of Brian and me. If he did those things, he did them outside of our sight and earshot. Like many parents, because of their love for their children, they kept their squabbles private, and did their best to perpetuate the image that everything about our family life was fine. Moreover, Mother felt compelled to "fix" whatever might be wrong; she went out of her way to maintain the impression that we were the "perfect" Christian family.

I had but one hint that something was awry. The one thing I knew for sure, Dad sometimes accused Mom of not putting the money he gave her in the bank. This was long before online banking, so it was relatively easy for Mother to keep Dad from knowing how much money we had on hand in our checkbook at any given time simply by concealing the bank statements. When Dad asked to see the statements, Mother told him—in my earshot, at times—that the bank statements weren't coming in, that there must be some mistake. All the while, she was secretly spending money from their bank account for her own purposes.

One afternoon, I walked into the downstairs extra bedroom and saw Mom hiding something under the mattress. The look on Mom's face revealed that she knew that she had been caught doing something she didn't want others to know.

"Mother, what are you doing?" I asked as I peered at her stuffing something between the mattress and the box spring.

"We hide our extra money there," she said, quickly replacing the mattress.

I've always had good intuition and have been fairly accurate in my hunches. When Mom left the house that day to go to the grocery store, I told Brian, "You watch the back door, and if you see Mom coming while I'm in the back bedroom, you yell to me."

Brian stood watch as I hurried to the extra bedroom. I hoisted the mattress up with my shoulder and felt the box spring beneath it. My hand landed on some envelopes and I carefully pulled them out.

Sure enough. The envelopes were filled with bank statements.

Because I knew about the money and the bank statements under the mattress, the prosecutors wanted me to testify in Mother's trial. They seemed convinced that the bank statements proved that Mother had access to the missing money and was using it in her efforts to hire someone to murder our dad.

CHAPTER 8

The Unprecedented Sentence

From the moment Mother was arrested, she was never any-thing but remorseful for her actions in setting the wheels in motion that resulted in the death of our dad. She immediately admitted her guilt. She made no attempt to escape the authorities, nor did she try to cover her tracks. From the beginning she did not want to go to trial and expose Brian and me to the sordid mess that had precipitated the situation that led to Dad's death. Rather than do that, she chose to keep quiet, to say nothing publicly about what she had experienced behind the closed doors of her marriage. Nor did she bring up anything in court about Dad's sexual liaisons with one of his coworkers. She didn't even want her attorneys to involve her family in her defense.

No, Mom would rather die than have all that dragged out for the world to see and hear. She always felt that everything in our family had to appear "happy," but she realized now that she couldn't fix this.

Consequently, she never took the stand in her own defense. Not even during the sentencing portion of her trial did she attempt to explain her actions. And her attorneys failed to bring up any mitigating circumstances that might help the jury understand how such a sweet, church-going woman, with the gentle features and quick smile, could have been driven to the point of risking her own life, as well as the children she was so desperately trying to protect, in hiring a man to murder our father.

In January 1986, almost one year to the day from when I had found my dad on the floor of our home, I was called to testify in court against my mother. I was the second witness called, the first being Grandfather Owens, my dad's father. I had just turned thirteen years of age.

Prior to testifying, I was sequestered in a room down the hallway from the courtroom, along with other witnesses and we were not permitted to talk. When I was called, I had to walk up an open corridor to get to the main doors of the courtroom. Walking up the hallway, as soon as we turned the corner, I was surrounded by cameramen and reporters pressing in on me, hurling loud, obnoxious questions at me. The bailiff and other legal staff quickly closed ranks around me, but I was shell shocked by the media frenzy and the hallway crowded with reporters covering the case.

When I walked in to the courtroom, I was surprised. I didn't know much about court procedures, but I assumed the courtroom would look similar to a Perry Mason type of situation, with dark wood paneled walls, and a large, comfortable chair behind a wall and a railing, sitting next to the judge's bench.

This courtroom was nothing like that.

I entered the courtroom through the main doors in the back of the room, and had to walk all the way around to the right, in front of the spectators attending this high profile case, and behind the attorneys' tables before I finally got to the front of the room. Mom and Sidney Porterfield—the man who had murdered my father—sat behind the attorneys, next to the railing.

The chair was right below the judge, but there was no wall surrounding me, just a swivel chair. I took my seat, and waited, doing my best not to look at my mother. The judge looked down and said something like, "You're going to be all right," in an odd attempt to set my mind at ease.

The prosecuting attorney wasted little time. After establishing my identity, he went straight to the damning evidence. "Now tell us about what you found under the mattress in the back bedroom."

Mother did not know what I was going to say.

In my peripheral vision, I saw my mother nervously adjust in her seat.

She sat in silence, a terrified expression on her face as I told about finding the missing bank statements under the mattress. Perhaps for the first time, Mom realized that I knew there was something not right about those hidden statements.

I answered a few more direct questions, and was dismissed. I walked out of the courtroom without looking at my mother. People later told me that Mother watched me leave, gazing lovingly after me, perhaps hopeful that I might return her look. I did not. I never wanted to see her face again.

As soon as I opened the back door, the media surrounded me. Cameras flashed in my eyes, causing me to squint, and reporters called out questions I had no intention of answering, not that I could have. I cowered in fear, trying to shield myself from their overbearing demands. "Look this way, Stephen." "How do you feel?" All the way back down the hall toward the elevator, the press followed me, hurling their queries toward me and the prosecutor's staff who accompanied me. When I finally reached the elevator and the doors whisked shut behind me, the incessant voices were still yelling out to me. I squeezed my eyes

shut and leaned against the back wall of the elevator, so glad to
be leaving that chaotic place. I never wanted to see a reporter or
a press photographer again. And for most of my life, I didn't.

Afterwards, Aunt Carolyn was waiting for me, and hurriedly
accompanied me to the car and away from the commotion.

The rest of the trial was a travesty of justice, but I did not
know that at the time. Few other people did, either.

Mom's childhood experiences in which she said she was
beaten and sexually abused were never mentioned. Her claimed
endurance of spousal abuse as an adult was never brought up. It
was 1986, and these emotional and psychological abuse types of
defense arguments rarely saw the light of day, much less were
they understood. They were unmentionable. Nor were Dad's
affairs ever presented in testimony before the jury. The case was
presented as a textbook capital crime, with Mom arranging to
have Dad killed so she could collect about $100,000 in insurance
money.

There was never any argument over Mother's guilt or innocence. She declared her guilt right from the start. But because
she never took the stand and testified on her own behalf, the jury
never heard any information that may have explained what had
driven her to the extreme measures she had taken. Nor were any
mitigating factors—things that might have caused the jury to
consider the penalty as too harsh—ever presented.

Mother's attorneys called only three witnesses to testify on
her behalf—Dr. Max West, the psychiatrist with whom she
had met for a mere one-hour session, and two women who had
worked alongside Mother in the Shelby County Jail, who testified that she was a good prisoner, who caused no problems, volunteered to work, and attended Bible classes while in jail. That
was it. That was the best they could do in a case that could take
her to the electric chair.

By their own admission and written time sheets attesting to the fact, Mom's attorneys spent only two hours preparing for the sentencing portion of her trial.

But had Mom's lawyers done a better job, had the issue of possible abuse been raised and questioned, had the letters—found in Dad's desk after his death—written by a woman who admitted having a sexual relationship with my father, been entered as evidence, had any of the mitigating factors been introduced to the jury during the sentencing phase, perhaps even one of the jurors might have voted against the death penalty. None did, although several visibly shaken jurors later said that they did not believe Mom deserved to die for this crime, but there were no other options presented.

Consequently, on January 15, 1986, Mom was sentenced to death. If carried out, her execution would be the first time a woman was executed in Tennessee in more than 180 years. Moreover, Mother was the only person in Tennessee history to agree to a life sentence, and then receive the death penalty.

From that point on, the attitude of my family was "Let the legal system take its natural course." Certainly, as in any death sentence in the U.S., multiple appeals can take place before the convicted person is actually executed, but apart from Carolyn testifying in the post-conviction appeal, my extended family members were completely uninterested in following the appellate process. Mom's attorneys took the required steps to appeal Mom's conviction and sentence, in hopes of getting some relief. That day in the courtroom was the last time I saw my mother for nearly twenty-five years. As far as I was concerned, she was already dead.

CHAPTER 9

Life in the Hole

Following her sentencing, Mother was taken back to Shelby County Jail, and then within a short time, she was transferred to the Tennessee Prison for Women, a maximum security facility located on the outskirts of Nashville. When she first arrived at TPW, she had no idea what to expect. She had some familiarity with the unsavory elements of life in jail, having served sixty days in a county jail for forgery. Then while awaiting trial for her role in Dad's murder, she had been incarcerated in the Shelby County Jail. But TPW was a different world. This was prison.

Shaking in fear when she got off the bus, Mother was met by serious-looking, armed, uniformed guards wearing brown pants and khaki shirts. The poker-faced guards ordered her through the door where she saw a wall of steel bars, and on the other side of the bars, a group of curious onlookers, including officers and prison guards peering at her as though she were a wild animal. They had heard that a death penalty inmate was arriving—TPW's first and only death penalty inmate—and they all wanted to see what Mother looked like. Apparently, they assumed she would be a deranged maniac, a monster filled with hate. The Warden of Treatment saw the mayhem, and hurried down the hall, screaming at the gawkers.

"What in the world are you all doing? She's *just* a female. Get back to work." She waited and watched as the crowd dispersed. The expression on the Warden's face remained firm, but she softened her tone slightly, as she turned to Mother and said, "I'm sorry. That should not have happened. Are you okay?"

Mother nodded, and quietly said yes.

Despite the token kindness, rules were rules, and Mother was ordered inside where she was "processed," strip searched, and issued TPW prison clothes. For an ultra-modest Christian woman who had grown up rarely wearing a bathing suit in mixed company, to be forced to stand naked in front of the processors while she was probed and prodded as the guards searched for contraband, and then poked with needles as she received her inoculations, was demeaning and dehumanizing. Mother moved as though in shock. Once she finished the processing, she was led out of the receiving area, and shuffled toward the segregation unit, moving with difficulty because her hands and feet were shackled.

Mother had no idea that she would be living alone, locked down in total isolation twenty-three hours of every twenty-four. She was taken to her "room," an eight foot by ten foot cement-block-walled cell with a barred window, a commode and sink unit, and a twin bed along the wall. She received her food through a twelve-inch by four-inch slot in the solid steel door. This would be her home until she was executed. She was permitted out for one hour each day for exercise, a shower, and if there was opportunity, phone calls.

Numerous other women at TPW had been sentenced to life in prison, and several had been sentenced to life without parole. But for a number of years, Mother was the only woman on TPW's death row. Because TPW did not have a stand-alone death row facility, Mom was incarcerated in isolation.

From the first day, Brett Stein, one of Mom's attorneys who had been brought in less than thirty days before her trial to replace Wayne Emmons who had withdrawn from the case, told her, "Don't worry, Gaile. We're going to get this changed. We'll have this fixed."

She had no idea what the attorneys meant, or how they could "fix" a death penalty, but she watched daily to see their faces or a letter in the mail, looking for something, any news of hope from the attorneys. Nothing came.

After about eight months in prison, Mother resigned herself to the fact that nothing was going to change; she was living the life she would live till the day she died.

At first, when she had access to a phone, Mother called her sister Carolyn, and sometimes talked with Brian and me. Before long, however, Aunt Carolyn informed Mom that we really didn't want to talk to her anymore. Occasionally, she received some news from her father, but that information was limited, mostly bits and pieces he'd heard through Aunt Carolyn. Aside from that, the only contact Mother had with our family was through our cousin Thelma.

Loving and kind, yet brutally honest, Thelma kept Mom informed about Brian and me, but she also told her straightforwardly that there was little hope of her seeing us. Mom never lost hope, but she accepted that as her new reality.

She prayed frustrated prayers, "God, if you truly love me, why don't you at least let me see my boys, and let me tell them that I love them?" Over time, her prayer changed to, "Lord, let me see them just one time. That's all I ask." Almost instinctively, Mother knew that she had to hang onto hope. If she ever lost hope of seeing her boys, she'd have no reason to live.

She beat herself up constantly, wondering, "Will I ever be loved again?" She could not imagine anyone else loving her when she could not even love herself. During the long, lonely hours, Mother had nothing but time, so she began to read the Bible. She had made a commitment to Jesus Christ as a child, but she really didn't have a solid relationship with Him. Most of her religious experience had been steeped in legalism—keep the rules, and everything will be fine. Break the rules, and reap the consequences.

After about a year in prison, the numbness wore off, reality set in, and Mother began to weep. By now she had learned that tears can be dangerous in prison, exposing a certain vulnerability, but no matter how hard she tried, she couldn't contain the tears.

One morning, Mother woke up and began crying and kept on crying. She cried almost nonstop for nearly eight hours. Lying on the floor, she called out to God, begging for His forgiveness. Though nothing about her circumstances changed, this was a turning point in Mother's life. She knew she could not bring Dad back or make everything okay, but she truly believed that God forgave her. Although she had little hope of ever being released from prison, and no assurance that she'd ever see Brian or me again, she at least had the hope that when she was executed, she would wake up in heaven.

In 1987, Mother was given a prison job, doing paperwork in a property cage, while two other inmates stocked the shelves. Other than the prison officers, the two inmates from the general population were the first and only other human contact Mom had for nearly a year. For the first six years of her sentence,

Mother was kept in the segregated section of the prison known as Unit 2.

Finally, she received a policy exemption that allowed her to live among the general population of the prison. Mom flourished, and became a trusted "employee" doing clerical work. It was the first time she had ever touched a computer and she was excited to learn a new skill.

During the next ten years, Mom moved with ease among the general population of the prison and became a quiet and dependable "favorite" of staff and inmates alike. She was elected to the Inmate Council and met monthly with the prison officials, serving as the elected voice of her fellow inmates. She also served on the Grievance board, a position nominated by inmates and selected by prison staff members.

Although permitted to have visitors, Mom welcomed very few. The only visitors she wanted to see were her family members and none of us ever showed up. Pastor Greer visited her once, after she had been incarcerated for more than a year. Most of the visitors on Mother's visitation list were elderly. She encouraged no others to come.

For a long time, Mom avoided chapel services. "Jail house religion," she discovered, was frowned upon inside. Yet she also saw the real thing, and longed for the fellowship she had once known in her church circles. She met Linda Knott, an elderly woman who had been working as a volunteer within the prison for years, and had earned the respect of both prison staff and inmates alike. Linda told her about MasterLife Bible Study, and Mother consented to attend.

Some of the Christians who regularly visited the prison and joined in the Bible study were from the Donelson, Woodmont, Judson, and New Hope Baptist churches, whose congregations had active prison ministry at the Tennessee Prison for Women.

Mother decided to join their church, though she assumed she would never see inside the sanctuary except through photos.

Although Mother had been baptized at age twelve, as her appeal process wound down and her execution loomed, she felt that she wanted to be re-baptized in prison. One of the men assisting in Mother's baptism in the prison chapel had been volunteering with MasterLife for nearly ten years. His name was Steve Wilson. The guards supervised the baptisms, because even the water hose was considered a Class-A tool that could be used in an escape attempt or in some other malicious manner.

Contrary to images of life "inside," Mom experienced relatively few incidents of violence, although she did encounter one inmate who hurled a bottle of hot sauce at another woman. The bottle shattered and the glass caused great concern to the guards, since the shards of glass could be used as a weapon. But it was quickly cleaned up and life went on. Another unstable woman hit a fellow inmate in the head with a steam iron. And then there was Christa Pike, also on death row . . . who brutally tried to murder another inmate. Pike was one of the few inmates at TPW who actually attempted an escape.

Mom not only became a model prisoner; she became one of the most beloved inmates in the facility. She was known for helping the younger women adapt, and diffusing difficulties among older inmates. At the time Mom arrived at TPW, the average age of the inmates was 32.4 years old; over the years, the age of the new inmates dropped dramatically, with many under the age of twenty-five. Juvenile young women were incarcerated at TPW as well, although they were kept in lock down, isolated from the main population until the girls turned eighteen. They were then thrust into the general population. If the teenagers weren't angry when they arrived at TPW, after spending a year or two or more in isolation, they would be, and then they were unleashed to the wolves.

Mom became a mentor and an encourager to many of the younger inmates.

"I just can't do this time."

"How much time have you got, honey?" Mom asked.

"Two years."

"Two years? It's going to be over before you know it."

"Well, Miss Gaile, how long have you been here?"

"Ten years . . . fifteen years . . . twenty years. . . ."

Mom's attitude was: Your time in prison is what you make it. And she wanted to make it productive. She lived each day with the hope that she would either walk out of prison or she would go to heaven from TPW. The death penalty hanging over her head could easily have fostered within her a "Who cares?" attitude, but Mother fought against it. Even when things didn't go her way, she held her tongue.

"Why don't you just go ahead and cuss them out?" some of her fellow inmates asked. "What do you have to lose?" implying that she was going to die anyhow. What did it matter? But to Mother, it mattered.

Although my mom could not possibly know it at the time, God had plans to reward her good behavior.

In 1993, Nashville based, singer-songwriter Marshall Chapman came to the prison to perform a free concert for the inmates. Marshall's songs have been recorded by a wide array of artists including Joe Cocker, Emmylou Harris, Jimmy Buffett, Tanya Tucker, Conway Twitty, Wynonna (Judd), and Olivia Newton-John. Mother was chosen to be a part of the "hospitality group" that would welcome the musician to TPW. Along with a couple other inmates, Mom delivered a fruit tray to Marshall "backstage" and the death row inmate and the famous song-writer struck up a conversation. They hit it off immediately, and within a short time following the concert, Marshall wrote back to Mom. They exchanged letters and continued writing to each other ever since.

One of the life-changing and life-saving relationships Mother established in prison was with Pat Williams, whom she met in 1998. Pat and her husband Gene visited the women's prison every Sunday night and helped with the MasterLife Bible Study group. When Mom first met Pat, she had little tolerance for "the lady who cried all the time." Indeed, a woman with a sensitive heart, Pat often taught through her tears. She had such compassion for the inmates; any time one of the women shared about her past, Pat began boo-hooing like a baby. Mom didn't go for all that. She had gone so far as praying, "God, please take away my tears," because she knew that tears were considered a weakness in prison.

For her part, Pat noticed the respect and high esteem the other inmates had for Mother. Even in Bible studies, the other women would look to Mother for approval when they spoke, to make sure what they were saying was okay.

Pat observed that the volunteers loved Mother, as well, and held her in high regard. Even the prison guards and officials had tremendous respect for Mother. The officers with whom Mother worked depended on her, often asking her opinion or advice about prison matters, but rarely risking Mom's displeasure by interrupting her visits with Pat and Gene.

After living for ten years in the general population, due to an administrative change in 2002, Mom was transferred back to Unit 3, the segregated, isolation of solitary confinement. She spiraled downward, and for a while even turned away from her friend, Pat. While in Unit 3, Mom felt angry, hurt, and abandoned. Finally, through a special concession, though she remained in Unit 3, Mother was allowed out of the segregated pod so that she could have a job and interact with other inmates in her Unit.

In what started as a means of giving hope to Mother, Pat said to her one day, "When you get out of here, you can come live with us." Pat's husband Gene picked up on the idea. During visits, he frequently quipped to Mom, "I was running the vacuum cleaner in your room today. I'll be glad when you get out of this prison so you can run the vacuum cleaner yourself."

Like Gene, Pat believed that, one day, Mother would walk out of the prison. She became even more convinced of that one night as she was leaving the prison, shortly after the Supreme Court decided against hearing Mother's case. It was a clear, star-lit evening, and as Pat exited the complex after visiting, she looked up toward the sky and asked, "God, what kind of hope can I offer Gaile? What should I say to her? What is the message for Gaile, if it all comes down to this?"

Pat was convinced that the Lord instructed her, "One day at a time, in the palm of My hand." That was His message for Mother.

The next time Pat visited Mother, she shared the message God had impressed upon her. But rather than receiving the word as comforting, Mother became angry, not at Pat, but at God. "Yeah, right. In the palm of Your hand, on a gurney."

Mother went back to her cell, but she couldn't shake what Pat had told her. She had come to respect Pat's spiritual insights, so whether Mother accepted the word or not, she knew it was genuine.

Mother prayed, "If you want me to stay in the palm of Your hand, You are going to have to have Pat help me to stay there."

That wasn't a problem for Gene and Pat. They had already promised Mother that they would be with her till the end— either the end of her sentence, or the end of her life. In talking about the possible execution, Pat had told Mother, "I am going to be there with you, no matter what."

Walking back to her cell in isolation, Mother imagined the execution chamber. She could envision the room with the extra heavy glass with the seals around the window, and the drawn curtain that was opened for the viewers of executions. She could not endure the thought of her friend sitting there behind the glass, watching her die. *Pat can't see that,* she thought. *I don't want anyone to see that. I want them to leave that curtain closed when I die.*

When Mom's hope was at its lowest point, she hurt Pat severely by trying to protect her from the pain of dealing with her impending death. Mom basically told Pat not to return to visit her. She felt strongly that her time at TPW was drawing to a close, and she did not want Pat to have to go through that. Almost instinctively, Mother knew that Pat would never give up on her; she had, after all, promised to be with her all the way to the end—even if the end was execution. "Why does she want to do this to herself?" Mom asked. So the only way to keep Pat from experiencing that pain was to drive her off.

Although Mother wasn't mean to Pat, she wrote her a rather brusque letter. "You don't need to come to see me anymore," she told Pat. "*Please* don't come anymore."

When Pat received the letter, she read it in her bedroom. She was not only hurt, she became angry. "I didn't spend all these years just wasting my time," she told Gene.

Nevertheless, Pat reluctantly backed off. For several weeks she made no attempt to see Mother. She and Gene visited other women and girls in the prison, but complied with Mom's request. But she was miserable not seeing Mom. A few weeks later, Gene was at the prison for a meeting so, without Pat's knowledge, he stopped to see Mother. "Gaile, you are not helping Pat," he said. "Please, think about letting her come to visit you."

Mom gave in. "Okay," she said. "If she wants to come, I will see her."

Pat returned to her usual routine of visiting with Mother. She was with her when nobody else was, encouraging her, praying for her.

"Had it not been for Pat," Mother said later, "I might have committed suicide."

Of course, for all those years, I knew nothing of Mother's circumstances in prison, and at that time in my life, I could have cared less whether she lived or died.

CHAPTER 10

Circled Wagons

After the murder, my immediate family members and our church family closed ranks around Brian and me, trying to protect us from the sordid details surrounding Dad's death. The relatives and friends did their best to help my brother and me deal with the horror. They meant well by extolling the virtues of our father. And although they probably never intended to do so, by their comments about Mother and their attitudes toward her unspeakable and unfathomable actions, they also watered the seeds of resentment planted in my heart by what I had seen that awful night, seeds that would soon grow into dense, monstrous, almost indestructible breeding grounds for hatred of my own mother.

I was so deeply hurt and emotionally devastated, I didn't ask many questions. The swirl of discussion focused on the immediate issue of where we were going to live, with Dad dead and Mother in prison. The uncertainty of where Brian and I were going to go, and how we were to function, pervaded my mind.

Dad is dead; Mom has been taken away. We've lost both of our parents. How are we going to live? Who is going to take care of us? It was bad enough having lost our dad, now we had lost our mom, as well. We had no idea where we might end up, and all sense of security was gone.

Grandpa Owens wanted to take Brian and me to live with him, but Grandmother Owens had just passed away in November, so that didn't seem like a good option. Some of our relatives in Arkansas were willing to have us, as well, but the Court determined it made the most sense for us to move in with Mom's younger sister and her husband, Aunt Carolyn and Uncle Joey, so we could continue living and going to school in Memphis. They gave me special permission to return to Alturia Elementary School for my sixth grade school year rather than changing schools after Dad's death.

Life with Aunt Carolyn and Uncle Joey was as good as could be expected. Aunt Carolyn's focus was on keeping the family together and maintaining a sense of normalcy. She continued taking us to church and facilitated our school activities. She poured herself into raising Brian and me the best way she knew how. She and Uncle Joey sacrificed a lot to take two young boys into their home. We never questioned their intentions or their love.

I moved quickly from grief and mourning over Dad's death to anger and bitterness when I discovered that Mom had been involved. Losing a loved one under any circumstances is always difficult for a family. Losing the pillar of strength in our family was tough enough; I was already reeling from dealing with the wrenching question of who could have done such a horrible thing to such a wonderful man, a loving father, my hero. But then to find out that the one person I trusted more than anyone in the world other than Dad was actually the one who had caused this horrific nightmare to occur sent me straight into an emotional quagmire. It would not be an exaggeration to say that in those months and years immediately following the murder, I hated my mother.

Because of my own emotional makeup, I worried more about Brian than I did about myself. I knew he was just as angry as I was, but we didn't verbalize it. We rarely spoke to each other about Mother or what she had done to our dad. Pastor Greer and Aunt Carolyn felt Brian and I needed to go to counseling. The money for counselors came from mom and dad's estate, governed by the court, and approved by Aunt Carolyn. The counseling sessions were helpful, but I quickly tired of answering questions about my feelings.

Feelings? I didn't have any *feelings*! I was numb. Didn't the counselor understand that the only way I could survive was to steel myself off from my feelings? I didn't want to talk about how I felt. I didn't want to think about how I felt. I didn't *know* how I felt; much less could I process those feelings.

Brian attended more sessions than I did, but after a few dead ends, I said, "I'm done. I'm not going to any more counseling. I can handle this by myself."

Aunt Carolyn didn't push the issue with me, and allowed me to make that decision. Curtailing the counseling may have made sense at the time, but over the years, I've seen the repercussions in my life, and have often wished that I would have stayed in counseling longer. I might have developed better ways to deal with the loss of my dad. Maybe I could have learned how to handle the hatred, bitterness, and resentment I felt toward my mom. Perhaps had I learned how to forgive, and better cope with my experiences, I would not have lived in my own personal prison for so long.

But I didn't. So the entire emotional sludge continued to stew beneath the surface of my life.

Within a few months after Brian and I moved in permanently with Aunt Carolyn and her husband, their marriage fell apart. Aunt Carolyn—who had never given birth to children of her own—was suddenly thrust into the tenuous position of raising two boys as a single mom with no child-raising experience. Brian and I were "all boy," so we taxed her patience at times, but Aunt Carolyn loved us, took good care of us, kept us fed and clothed, and she kept us in church.

Although Aunt Carolyn had our best interests at heart, there was some natural tension as we floundered through these new relationships, especially as Brian and I grew into our teenage years.

Prior to Dad's death and Mom's incarceration, I had attended public schools at Alturia Elementary. Later, I moved to First Assembly Christian School, a private school where I completed my remaining middle school and high school education.

I didn't correlate my negative actions or attitudes to Mother's deeds, but I was still angry and bitter. At school, any time someone asked me about my family, I replied succinctly and tersely, "My mom hired somebody to kill my dad." That was it. I offered no other information, and few people pushed me for more. Dad was on a pedestal in my mind, and Mother was in prison. That said it all.

I often wondered what it would have been like to have Dad at my ball games, or to be able to go out and play golf with him as we had when I was younger. Sometimes I'd get deeply emotional because Dad wasn't there in the stands at my basketball games. Whenever I missed Dad so intensely, the usual emotional reaction within me was to become even more resentful toward my mother who had robbed me of Dad's presence in my life.

Although I didn't know it at the time, my cousin Thelma kept Mom informed about Brian and me. She even sent Mom a photograph of us that became one of Mother's most treasured possessions in prison. Over the years, as Brian and I grew up, Aunt Thelma sent our school pictures to Mom. Brian and I never did.

Thelma was actually a first cousin to Mom and a second cousin to me. She was much older than I was, never married, and seemed almost grandmotherly in her care for Brian and me. She worked as a Memphis high school principal, eventually moving into a position with the city's Board of Education. She instilled within me a great love for education, and inspired me to pursue a career as a teacher.

She drove a huge Cadillac and spoiled Brian and me terribly. She called us often at Aunt Carolyn's house and watched out for us constantly. Brian and I took several vacations with Thelma to Destin, Florida, and other getaways. She loved us dearly, and in some ways, became a type of surrogate mother, along with Aunt Carolyn, filling some of the void in our lives because our own mother was gone.

I rarely asked about Mother, but occasionally her name surfaced in a conversation, especially when someone in the family heard about another appeal in her case. I didn't know or care much about Mother's legal appeals, but when the matter came up, the consistent message I heard from relatives was that Mother was running Dad's name into the ground through her appeals process. That made me even angrier at her. It was bad enough that she had set in motion the death of my father; now she wanted to grind his reputation into the dirt, too. That was the way it was always presented to me, and that's the way I interpreted Mother's actions for more than twenty years.

During my high school years, resentment and anger fomented in me perpetually, but I also felt a strong responsibility to help protect and care for my younger brother. Three and a half years separated us so I kept a watchful eye out on Brian, making sure that he was okay. Brother Greer's sons-in-laws, Roy and Bud, tried to be male role models for Brian and me, and they provided a good influence. I loved those guys, and I appreciated that they expressed their opinions about how I acted and felt, but didn't look down on me whenever I made mistakes.

Brian and I had received a small inheritance from Mom and Dad's estate, but because we were so young when we moved in with Aunt Carolyn, the money was put into trust funds for each of us until we were of age. When either of us needed money for new clothes, medical or dental expenses, or in my case, for a car during my later teens, we went to Aunt Carolyn, because the court had given her supervisory control over the money eventually to be inherited by Brian and me. But every major transaction in the meantime had to be approved by the judge. For instance, because Brian and I attended a private Christian school, those fees had to be requested by Aunt Carolyn on our behalf and approved by a judge each year. The same was true for other major expenditures.

At several points during my teen and young adult years, Pastor Greer encouraged me that it might be a good idea to visit my mom in prison. He never pressured me, but he emphasized that he felt that it would be emotionally and spiritually healthy for me to stay in touch with Mother.

Brother Greer told me, "Stephen, everybody makes mistakes, and your mom is still your mother. You are still her son. You need to get to a place where you can go see her."

"I have no desire to see her," I responded, barely covering my bitterness.

"Well, you'll get there someday," the pastor conceded hopefully, without further effort to convince me.

I disagreed. I had no desire to see Mother. That was the last thing I wanted to do. In fact, in candid conversations whenever someone asked me about her, I responded vehemently, "It's a good thing she's in prison, because if I saw her, I'd kill her."

In retrospect, I doubt strongly that I would have taken physical revenge against my mother, but my intense anger toward her seethed perpetually, and rather than diminishing with time, the pain and resentment festered, scarred, and split wide open again. Not surprisingly, I soon sought ways to dull the pain.

I did a lot of partying in high school, trying to drown my anger and resentment, acting as though I was enjoying myself. I was longing for something, anything that felt even half-way good.

I played high school basketball and found acceptance with my peers through sports. But with my friends off the court, I quickly succumbed to the temptation to drink. Oddly enough, I bypassed beer and went straight for the hard stuff, drowning my sorrows with my friend "Jack Daniels."

During my senior year, I settled down and tried to improve my grades so I could get into college. For the most part, I did much better. Until our senior trip.

For our graduation trip, we went to Nassau, Bahamas. Although all of the students were from a Christian school, my roommates and I went to Paradise Island, visited the gambling casinos, and managed to find a place to buy alcohol and bring it back to our hotel rooms.

We got in big trouble for going to Paradise Island, but I was still allowed to graduate with my class.

Regardless of my inner turmoil and my external shenanigans, I returned to church every week. I sometimes felt convicted of my wrongdoing, but I sought forgiveness and moved on. Somewhere buried beneath all the rubble in my heart, I knew that if God could forgive me for my sins, He could also forgive my mother, but I never gave that possibility much thought.

After my high school graduation, I enrolled at the University of Memphis where I hoped to earn my bachelors degree in Physical Education. I loved sports and like my dad, I enjoyed coaching. I was also fascinated by science, and inspired by Thelma's example, I really wanted to be a teacher.

Throughout my college years, I continued my attempts to dull my inner pain with alcohol. Aunt Carolyn disapproved of drinking, but she also realized that she was powerless to keep me from doing it, if I really wanted to.

Over the years, Mom tried to communicate with Brian and me by sending cards and letters to us at Aunt Carolyn's address. I recall receiving a few of such notes from Mom, but not many. Perhaps Aunt Carolyn decided that receiving letters from prison was not in our best interests.

During the earliest years of Mom's incarceration, she was permitted an occasional phone call to family. She called Brian and me at Aunt Carolyn's home and we talked to her briefly, always in curt, stilted statements.

On one occasion, Mom asked Aunt Carolyn if she thought her calls were upsetting us. "What do you mean by *upset?*" Aunt Carolyn responded coolly. "The truth is, Gaile, the boys don't want to talk to you." Mother stopped calling after that, but apparently, she continued sending notes and cards, especially for our birthdays and holidays.

Some people say time heals all wounds. I don't believe that. As I grew older, rather than time taking away the pain, it exacerbated it. My resentment increased exponentially as I realized that Mother had *allowed* me to walk into our house that night in 1985. When I thought about it, I got furious. Sometimes it hit me with such force I could barely stand it. Not only had Mother been involved in Dad's death, *she let me walk into it!* Why? How could you, Mother?

Even if she had set the wheels in motion to have my father murdered, surely she could have prevented Brian and me from entering the house that night. "Stay in the car boys, until I go unlock the door." Or, she could have gone in first. But she hadn't.

In later years, Mom said that she had asked Porterfield not to carry out the horrible deed for which she had initially attempted to hire him. But he had. And when she came home with us that night, she was as horrified as Brian and I were. Maybe so. But if there was even a hint that something might be wrong, why did she allow me to experience the nightmare first?

Whether or not Mother's assertion that she had no advance notice of the crime was true, the nightmare existed in my mind. Because of Mom allowing me to go into the house first, I've lived with the horror of those visions of what I saw for nearly three decades. I still do and I guess, in some ways, I always will.

CHAPTER 11

A Red-Haired Angel

While pursuing my college degree, I also worked at a job with a charter bus service for several years. One weekend, I had taken a tour group to Branson, Missouri, when Lisa Kennedy showed up in our home church in Memphis on Sunday morning. Lisa's family had known my family for years, and we had all attended the same church. Lisa and I had gone to the same summer church camps. Although she was a few years younger than me, we had grown up together and had many mutual friends. Then Lisa's family had moved away to Nashville. Now she was back to attend the University of Memphis. Aunt Carolyn was excited to see Lisa and made a point to talk with her after the service.

That night, Aunt Carolyn called and left a message telling me that Lisa had been at the church that morning. I could tell she was playing matchmaker, but I didn't mind; Lisa piqued my interest. I was home the following Sunday, and as soon as I spotted Lisa in church, I knew I wanted to ask her out. We talked briefly after the service, and we went to lunch along with Aunt Carolyn and Pastor Greer and his family. Three days later, I called Lisa for a real date. We went out to eat at Applebee's restaurant. A few months later, we were engaged to be married.

Our relationship was easy and natural. I was twenty-two years old, and Lisa was twenty. We had known each other since childhood, so Lisa knew my story, the good and the bad of it. We had lived less than a mile apart and her school bus went past our home on Scepter Drive every morning. Her parents were also well aware of my family history.

Shortly after we began dating, Lisa and her family went on vacation to Hawaii. Lisa called me from Hawaii every single day, and this was well before inexpensive long-distance calling plans. Before she got home, everybody in the church knew that Lisa had called me. Word traveled quickly in our congregation. Everyone in the church circles was excited for Lisa and me, seeing us as an ideal couple. That was the good news. The bad news? We couldn't do anything without feeling as though our lives were under a microscope.

Lisa and I talked about everything without reservations, so when any subject about my parents was mentioned, we discussed it freely and openly. Lisa recognized that I felt as though I owed everybody a huge debt for helping to guide me through the tumultuous times following Dad's death. Part of that was real— I genuinely did feel a sense of gratefulness to Aunt Carolyn and the church folks who had been so protective of Brian and me—but another part of that was a feeling that was imposed on me by certain people in the church, giving me a not-so-subtle impression that I did indeed owe them for all they had done for my brother and me. The resulting obsession with trying to please the people of the church, and my reluctance to confront them even when I disagreed with their opinions was warped and unhealthy.

Lisa and I were so comfortable with one another, even though we were both still in college working on our degrees, we felt ready to marry. When I asked her father for her hand in marriage, he had but one request, that one of us finish our college education before the wedding day. So although I asked Lisa to marry me before attending a First Assembly's football game in October 1995, we didn't get married until February 1997, after Lisa had received her college degree. I was still working on mine.

We had originally thought about getting married around Valentine's Day, but then recognized that a wedding date so close to the anniversary of Dad's death may not be such a good idea. We settled on February 1 instead.

Lisa preferred a small, intimate wedding, and probably would have been just as happy to elope, but I knew the people of the church would be terribly disappointed if we didn't invite the congregation. Before long, our invitation list exceeded five hundred people.

We got married on an unseasonably warm day in early February. Mom's initiating Dad's murder was always the elephant in the room even on Lisa's and my wedding day. It never went away and loomed behind every relationship. Many of my groomsmen, for example, were best friends with my dad, so there was no escaping my past.

Not surprisingly, I couldn't help thinking how proud Dad would have been on Lisa's and my wedding day, how much he would have enjoyed being there with me. There I was, with some of his best buddies, standing at the front of the church. The only person missing was Dad. Ironically, it didn't really strike me that Mother would have been excited to have been there, as well. My attitudes toward Mother had changed little over the years.

I had not always dealt well with the anger that seethed below the surface in my life. I carried a lot of baggage into Lisa's and my marriage. There were emotional issues I had never worked through. Strong as it was, my anger even helped me to cover up other things with which I struggled, and as long as I was protected by family and friends within the church, I could control the emotional issues easier without ever resolving them. But that didn't mean they went away. They were still there, percolating below the surface, the pressure building like a volcano that could blow at any moment.

Without even realizing it, I harbored all sorts of trust issues. How could I trust Lisa, or any other woman for that matter, when the woman I had trusted the most in the world had betrayed not only me, but our entire family? If you can't trust your own mother, who can you trust?

Before we were married, Lisa had as good of an understanding as possible of the pressures with which I lived, but she hoped that we might be able to operate differently once we were husband and wife. Adding to the stress of living in the shadows of a murder were the unexpected, uninvited, and definitely unappreciated visits by lawyers who simply showed up at our doorstep out of nowhere, attempting to convince me to become involved in Mother's court case appeals. I was not interested and bluntly told the attorneys so.

I had already been disillusioned by such attorney visits even before Lisa and I were married. While I was still living with Aunt Carolyn, a couple of attorneys had asked for a meeting with our family and Pastor Greer. We consented to the meeting and immediately regretted it. The two lawyers, one male and one female, attempted to get our family to sign a document asking to reduce Mother's sentence from a death sentence to life in prison. The attorneys tried every trick in the book to make our family feel guilty for not going to bat for Mother. They especially tried to shame Brian and me into signing. "Well, don't you love your mom? Do you just want your mom to die?"

They just couldn't get it through their heads that nobody wanted to be involved, that our family had made a decision early on to allow the judicial system to take its course. It wasn't merely a "whatever will be, will be" attitude. We refused to defend Mother's actions and the attorneys' attempted coercion pushed everyone in the wrong direction. At one point, the male lawyer looked at Brian and me and said, "We just want this to be a win-win situation."

Brimming with bitterness, Brian looked back at him and said, "Well, unless you can raise up our dad from the grave, it is not going to be a win for us." The meeting ended badly, and we came away even more convinced that Mother was merely attempting to manipulate matters, and that she was willing to drag Dad's reputation through the mud to save her own hide.

Once Lisa and I married, the surprise visits continued. I emphatically told Lisa, "I do not want to talk to those people. If they come to the door, don't even answer." Lisa understood and did her best to fend off the attorney contacts.

Not surprisingly, Lisa and I went through some intensely difficult times during the early years in our marriage despite my previous negative experience with professional counseling. We sought help from two marriage counselors, as well as Pastor Greer, working together to put our relationship back on track. It was there, in that most intimate of relationships that God revealed more to me about forgiveness, my need to forgive, as well as my need to be forgiven.

Many of my initial ideas about forgiveness were conditional. I was willing to forgive based on certain criteria. If the person looked and sounded remorseful, or said the right magic words, I was willing to forgive. If the person came back and said he was sorry in a convincing manner, and made restitution as much as possible, he should be forgiven. In my estimation, some offenses were "forgivable" and others were not.

Now, God was convicting me that my "situational forgiveness" was not forgiveness at all. I wasn't really forgiving Mother from my heart. To me, forgiveness was situational, to be applied—or not—according to the circumstances, but God was showing me that if I did not forgive totally, I was not really forgiving at all. I couldn't pick which offenses I would forgive and what I would not forgive. If I was going to forgive, I knew I had to let go of all that.

There were several layers of forgiveness I had to work through. God got me to a point where I had to make a decision about what was more important—continuing to be angry or having a relationship with Him? Continuing to be bitter or reestablishing some sort of relationship with my mother?

In true forgiveness, you don't forget what the person who wounded you did; you don't condone the actions of the person who hurt you. But you don't have to continue living there, either. I realized that I would wake up every morning without a father in my life, and that would not change. But I could make some choices regarding my attitude toward my mother.

It was a turning point in my willingness to forgive my mother when I could let go of it. That wasn't easy, and there were times when I simply had to grit my teeth and grind through my feelings. But forgiveness was a choice that had to begin in my heart.

When Lisa and I decided to rebuild our marriage on a foundation of love, forgiveness, and absolute truthfulness, we decided to start fresh and move to Nashville.

When we talked to others about moving away, it was extremely difficult for me because of my loyalty to the people who had helped me. I felt that I still owed a debt, and it was a huge weight on my shoulders.

Not surprisingly, Lisa's and my moving away was not considered wise by many family and church members. But I felt it was paramount to do what was best for us, and we needed a clean start. I constantly had people in my ear, offering their advice, and ironically, nobody suggested that getting away from the memories in Memphis might be good for us.

It was difficult for both of us to leave, but it was especially a struggle for me; nevertheless, we pulled up our roots, and moved from Memphis to Nashville. Within a few weeks of moving, I looked at Lisa and said, "Why didn't we do this a long time ago?" We still loved our family and friends back in Memphis, but moving away was like a breath of fresh air for us. It was an opportunity for a fresh start.

We moved to Nashville in May and during our first year in the Nashville area, Lisa and I went through nearly every major life-change event a young couple can experience. Besides working to overcome the tension in our relationship, we had close family members pass away, financial stress, and job changes for me. We had just bought our first house. Then my dear cousin Thelma passed away in August.

We found out in September 2000, that we were going to have a baby, but Lisa had a miscarriage at eleven weeks—the day before Thanksgiving—and we lost our first child. We felt emotionally devastated. "What's going on here, God?" we prayed. "We've come through so much already and now this?" Lisa's parents were nearby and were wonderfully supportive, but she and I knew we had to walk through this pain together.

We were discouraged and nearly ready to give up. We wallowed in despair and depression for a while. One day, Lisa and I were talking, and I said, "Lisa, we have to get up and move on." To break out of our depression, we tried to get out of the house more frequently; we took walks around the neighborhood in the evenings. Anything to bring some sense that we could survive.

We had already endured a rough year and then experienced another severe blow when my grandmother passed away in December as a result of breast cancer.

What next? I had gone through my own issues with my dysfunctional family. Lisa and I had struggled with our own issues. Every time I felt as though we were coming up for air, something else hit us and weighed us down. I punished myself by thinking about the "what ifs," what if I had done this or that? I questioned God rather vehemently. "Lisa was already discouraged by the miscarriage. Why did we have to go through more difficulties?" I soon realized that I wasn't really saying "we" but I was asking "Why me? Why are you allowing this to happen to *me?*"

Certainly, there were points where I felt like walking away from God and forgetting Him entirely, especially during the early years following Dad's death. My prayers of frustration sounded something like this: "God, You've taken my family from me already. And it took a long time for me to feel okay again, and now Lisa and I have had our problems. I'm really tired of it."

But I found myself asking the same sort of question the apostle Peter had asked: "Where else is there to go? You are the only One who offers any hope."

For a while, Lisa and I were constantly trying to pick each other up, stumbling from one day to the next, wondering what might hit us next. At times, I questioned, *Where is God in all of this? And what good is faith in God anyhow? Is this the best I can hope for in life?*

When I hit those rock bottom, ebb tide moments, something inevitably happened to turn my attention back to God. Admittedly, I was sometimes driven to God out of sheer desperation; I didn't know what else to do or where else to go. My nakedly honest prayers held little back. "God, I'm mad at You, but I don't know what else to do. I feel as though I'm lost in the woods, and I've always been told that if I'm lost, but I trust in

You, that You will direct my paths. But part of my problem is *You!*"

God didn't punish me for my blunt expressions of exasperation, but He didn't placate my lack of faith, either. He was teaching me some important principles, and like any good teacher, He knew I couldn't grasp the entire course in one lesson. Although my faith was weak at times, it was nonetheless genuine. I still believed that my heavenly Father loved me and had a good future for me. He didn't have to give me supernatural signs in the heavens or speak to me from a burning bush. Just His letting me know, "You're going to be all right" was enough to keep me going.

Throughout this time, I didn't confide in many people. As far as I was concerned, Lisa and I were in the battle together and we were either going to make it together or we would crumble under the pressure together. We didn't go to all of our friends, neighbors, or even fellow believers at our church. We knew we had to make this journey together or not at all. Nor would I contact anyone in Memphis with whom we formerly had close relationships.

On the positive side, our isolation forced Lisa and me to talk openly and to communicate honestly about what we were thinking and feeling. It bonded our relationship in a way that may not have happened any other way. We felt that no matter what happened, together, with Christ in the center of our relationship, we could handle anything. We simply took our concerns to God, and said, "Okay, God. What do you want us to do?"

When we didn't know what to do next, we waited. Patience wasn't one of our stronger suits, but slowly we were learning that the timing was in God's hands. I'd be reminded of that lesson many times and in many different ways over the next few years.

CHAPTER 12

It Started with Zachary

We found out that we were pregnant again in early February 2001.

At first we were overjoyed, but we were also apprehensive going into the second pregnancy, so we were especially cautious and careful. Right from the beginning, though, we received another shock to our systems. Testing showed that there was a chance that our child could have Down's syndrome, so once again our emotions bounced all over the board.

Lisa's doctor ordered an advanced ultrasound and the monitor revealed some positive, encouraging feedback, but we still weren't certain if our baby had Down's. The doctor suggested an amniocentesis test to check for abnormalities, but Lisa didn't want to risk having the amnio, because the procedure itself could increase the possibility of miscarriage. We decided that we were going to have the child and love the baby regardless. To us, abortion was not an option.

When Lisa went into labor, I prayed the entire time. Our son, Zachary Stephen Owens, made his debut on October 31, 2001. He weighed in at eight pounds, five ounces, and grabbed our hearts immediately. I was thrilled when I first heard the baby cry. I paced anxiously as the nurses took Zachary out to the nursery to clean him up and do the initial tests.

"Please, God," I prayed, "let him be okay." I was happy and excited, but nervous, as well. Finally, the nurses completed their exams. Zachary was fine, they declared.

He sure looked fine to Lisa and me; he was our own "miracle baby." Every time I looked at our beautiful baby boy—with his perfectly formed tiny fingers and toes; his tufts of soft, fine hair; his cherub cheeks—I gave thanks to God for a healthy baby. I was ecstatic and delighted to be a dad.

Having a baby caused me to recognize even more the roles of both parents in a child's life. I knew that, barring any tragedy, Lisa was always going to be there for our child, and I would be, too. Seeing how Zachary was so instantly attached to Lisa occasionally prompted thoughts about my own mother and her absence in my own life. *She is alive.* I thought. *So at what point is the bitterness and resentment just not worth it?*

As I gazed into Zachary's barely open eyes, it hit me that most of what this little guy was going to learn about life—at least the most important things—he would learn from Lisa and me. It struck me that just as I had learned from my dad, Zachary would learn from me, and no doubt, my attitudes about God, love, marriage, family, faith, and—oh, yes—forgiveness, would have a profound influence on shaping Zachary's values. What he would see in me might be even more important than what he might see and hear from his peers as he grew up.

Looking at our newborn baby boy, I realized that more than anything in life, apart from being a godly man and a good husband to Lisa, I wanted to be a good father for our son. And

I couldn't help wondering that if, despite the tensions and financial pressures he and Mom were experiencing about the time of my birth, my dad had felt the same way about me.

Lisa's mom and dad were equally ecstatic at the birth of Zachary. As I saw the excitement in their faces, I reflected just a little, as I imagined how Mother and Dad might have enjoyed this experience with us, had things been different.

Bittersweet as it was, I felt it was incumbent upon me to at least inform Mother about Zachary's birth, and that perhaps I ought to let Mother know that she was now a grandmother. Maybe that's what prompted me to send Mother a Christmas card eight weeks later—the first written message I had sent to her in fifteen years.

It wasn't a fancy card. The exterior depicted an angel heralding the news of Christ's birth by blowing a trumpet, with the words, "A Christmas Blessing to a Dear Mother." Inside I included a simple and brief handwritten note:

> Mom, I just wanted to wish you a Merry Christmas. I also wanted to introduce you to Mr. Zachary Stephen Owens. This is our first son born on Oct. 31, 2001. He weighed 8 lbs, 5 ounces. He is now 8 weeks old. He weighs 9 pounds. I hope you enjoy the pictures.
> Love ya,
> Stephen, Lisa & Zachary

I enclosed some pictures of Zachary and mailed the card right before Christmas 2001. Mom received it on Christmas Eve.

She responded within days. Along with a blanket she had somehow purchased for baby Zachary, she sent a brief note:

> You cannot imagine the joy I felt upon receiving the first Christmas card from you. The card was so beautiful. Then to hear from you the birth of Zachary was so overwhelming

*to me. I could not stop crying from joy! This made my
Christmas and the best one I have had.*

She thanked me for sending the pictures of Zachary and
showed no reluctance to ask for more.

*Just know that I can't have enough photos of Zachary,
so when you have extras, please send them to me. The truth
of the matter is I can't have enough photos of any of you. So
please anytime you have extras, please don't forget me.*

She closed her letter with a poignant statement:

*Know that I love you and you are continuously in my
prayers. Thanks from the bottom of my heart for sharing
your joy of Zachary with me.
My Love Always,
Mom*

As I read the simple note, it struck me that it could have
come from any mom, whether writing to her son in college or
in the military or merely living in another part of the country.
There were no indications of prison; no statements hinting at
her whereabouts or the conditions in which she was living. It
was odd, yet somehow refreshing that the focus of our first communications was not on prison-life. We had Zachary to thank
for that.

I didn't write back to her immediately. Indeed, I didn't write
again until February 22, 2002, after dragging through another
wrenching anniversary of Dad's death. Lisa noticed that every
year about the middle of February my mood and demeanor
became more contemplative, and at times, downright gloomy. I
never really emphasized the anniversary; I did nothing to com-
memorate the date; in fact, I tried to concentrate more on the
happy anniversary of Lisa's and my marriage, and Valentine's
Day that we celebrated that month, as well.

But February 17, 1985 was always there, ingrained in my heart and mind.

Nevertheless, nearly two months later, I sat down and wrote Mother a brief note, barely a paragraph or two long. I told her that Zachary was growing well and quickly, and that we would be dedicating him to the Lord in a ceremony at church in April. I didn't even hint that we would miss Mother's not being there for the dedication of her first grandson. Instead, I passed along other family news, that my brother Brian was engaged to marry his fiancée Staci in May, so I bragged on him a bit.

Mom, you would be so proud of Brian. He has done well for himself. He is a great young man. I know I'm not telling you anything you already didn't believe.

Recalling that Aunt Carolyn had discouraged Mother from writing or calling Brian and me years ago, I wanted Mother to know that although she was welcome to write, I needed healthy boundaries and had other priorities.

Before I go, I just want you to know that you can write anytime to us. I will make every attempt to return with a letter. But as you know, having a baby takes all of your day and night.

I paused for a moment, thought of the woman sitting on death row to whom I was writing, and then typed words that were fraught with meaning—both in what they said, and what they did not say:

Mom, no matter what, I will always love you.
I hope to hear from you soon.
Love always,
Stephen, Lisa & Zachary

Mom sent back an Easter card, along with a five-page hand-written note, although not as soon as she had hoped. The prison commissary was out of stamps so she had to wait until they received a new supply. In her note, Mom echoed some of the news I had sent her. "I do understand how little Zachary keeps you and Lisa busy, day and night." She then unwittingly, yet ironically added: "Parenting is a full time job . . . one with so much joy . . . so many blessings."

Ouch. As I read her note, it would have been easy to fire back, "Yes, Mother you are right. Parenting *is* a full time job! And it is not supposed to end when your kids are twelve and eight years of age." But she was obviously not thinking in those terms, so I took her words in the humble and conciliatory spirit I thought she had written them.

She continued, "Stephen, thanks for telling me I can write and that you will answer when you can. I don't expect you to take a lot of time away from your family to write. Just know anytime I hear from you will be wonderful. Even if it is just, 'Hi!'"

Mom then closed her note, saying, "Please hug Zachary every day for his Granny Gaile." It was the first time she had used that term of endearment, and it stuck. In time, Mother would shorten "Granny Gaile" to "G.G." and rather than Grandmother, Grandma, Nanna, or some other name, she became known to our Zachary, and eventually, our second son, Joshua, as "G.G."

My next communication with Mom was not until Mother's Day. Maintaining a warm but superficial tone, I told her briefly about Zachary's baby dedication and then I turned the letter over to Lisa to ask Mom about my medical background as a child. This would become a practice, too, in which I would write a paragraph or two, and then let Lisa continue on. I was glad to keep the lines of communication open with Mother, but I really didn't have much to say. It seemed odd almost to be so familiar with someone who in many ways was a stranger to me.

Mom wrote a return letter the same day she received our card. She seemed delighted to fill in Lisa about the details of my childhood, telling her all about my allergies, my inability to keep food down as a baby, and how I'd only eat carrots if she pureed and cooked them with no seasoning.

The level of personal contact we had with Mother at the time was enough for me. Actually, even that little contact with Mom was a stretch for me, but I wanted her to know about Zachary, and perhaps, someday, I may even tell him about her. Our communication with Mom was moving along at a somewhat comfortable, almost platonic pace. There was no mention of Dad, and few references to Mom's prison existence. An outsider reading our letters would never have imagined that these letters were between a mother on death row—convicted of being an accessory to the fact in murdering her own husband—and her son, who discovered his Dad's beaten body. Granted, the information exchanged was at a relatively superficial level, but the letters had a certain sweetness to them.

And then someone from the public defender's office showed up.

CHAPTER 13

Guilty, But Forgiven

Not long after Lisa and I began corresponding with my mother, I was in the shower when someone rang the doorbell. Lisa was holding baby Zachary in her arms, so she looked out the window before answering. To her surprise, she saw a marked government car in front of the house and an official-looking woman standing on our front porch.

When Lisa opened the door, the woman said hello, gave her name, and identified herself as being an investigator from the Federal Public Defenders Office now handling the Gaile Owens case, as she handed Lisa a business card.

An investigator? What could she want, other than to try to involve us in my mom's case, and we still had a foul taste in our mouths from the attorneys who had attempted to badger us when we lived in Memphis. We moved to Nashville to get away from our past; Lisa and I certainly did not welcome this intrusion.

It was an intensely warm day and the sun was blazing hot at the front of our house. Whether she was warm or merely using whatever tactic she thought might work, the investigator actually caught Lisa off guard and asked to step inside out of the heat to speak with her for just a second.

Lisa was irritated but allowed the investigator to step into our entry hall. Lisa told the woman that I was unavailable to speak, but that did not deter her. She asked if Lisa would talk with her instead. Apparently, the investigator was hoping that she might elicit my support by convincing my wife to talk to me or offer some kind of insight. Her questions seemed to beg for understanding of why the family would not help at all in the efforts to keep Mother from being executed.

The more the investigator probed, the more irritated Lisa became. She repeated the same answer to every question. "I am here to support my husband," Lisa said again and again, "so please respect our privacy."

The investigator pressed Lisa to ask me to speak with her. Extremely uncomfortable leaving the woman alone downstairs in our home, Lisa ran upstairs, still carrying Zachary, and quickly repeated all of this to me, even though she already knew what my answer would be. True to form, when Lisa presented the investigator's request, I responded, "No way, I don't want to talk."

Lisa went back downstairs and relayed my refusal. At that point, the investigator's demeanor changed. She seemed defensive and frustrated. "I have never seen a family show such a lack of interest!" she said, making no attempt to hide her exasperation.

Lisa said not another word to her, and simply showed her to the door.

Over the years, occasionally, other investigators and attorneys showed up on our doorstep unannounced, wanting me to help them with Mother's case. I consistently refused to talk with them. This time I had had enough!

I wrote a brief letter to Mother in prison, demanding that she call off the dogs. I wanted no part of talking to them.

My letter about the investigator's visit to our home prompted a quick response from Mother. In a plaintive tone, printed in all capital letters in Mother's own handwriting, she said,

> Hon, this letter is for no other purpose than to apologize for the intrusion in your life by the office that represents me in my legal appeals.
>
> I had not asked, nor do I think they need to see any of you. This has been done before and against my wishes at that time also.
>
> They came to see me today and told me they had attempted to talk to you, Brian, and Aunt Carolyn. I have put in writing to them that they are not to contact any of you again.
>
> I don't know if you know or even care what they are trying to do. I will give you a brief explanation and leave it at that. First they are not trying to get me out of prison or say I'm not guilty. As sad as it is and it hurts to admit I am responsible for "putting the wheels in motion" which ultimately resulted in Ron's death. I did try to stop and thought I had, which justifies absolutely nothing. When it came time to go to trial, I tried to plead guilty and be given a life sentence so no one (most especially you, Brian and family) had to go through trial. The judge would not accept my guilty plea and life sentence because co-defendant (man who killed Ron) would not do the same. He insisted on a trial. So ultimately the trial and death penalty. Not allowing me to plead guilty, which would have given me a life sentence, is the reason why it was unconstitutional and so my attorneys are appealing this sentence part and nothing

more. They are asking for life sentence. At some point they think it will help to have letters from family asking or in support of this. This may or may not be needed. They are totally blown away that Carolyn has maintained she wants me executed/dead, etc. In all of their professional careers, they've never had immediate family take this view or stance. Most families want prison/incarceration but not death penalty. But this is her view apparently, and I will respect this. So, I don't know your or Brian's view and will never ask.

While explaining this, let me explain to you that should the court ever give me this sentence, this is how it would work. Sentence of life would be effective date granted, not retro to 1986. All years I've been incarcerated (seventeen at this time) would be dead time. The very earliest I'd be eligible for parole would be after doing thirty years (2034). Being eligible doesn't mean you'd be granted parole, just go before Parole Board for consideration. At this time, I'd be eighty years old (I'll be fifty in Sept.). Reality is I will either die of old age in here or at the hands of the state by execution. I accepted this reality years ago.

I don't want to be executed. I'd not be honest if I said I did. I don't want any of you to face, see or witness the "media circus" that will come with execution. Whatever way I die, I am at peace. I do not fear dying. I am heaven bound!

I will do all I can to protect you from attorneys. I will never write a letter such as this again, unless you were to ask questions. I will write exact letter to Brian and Carolyn. My apology seems so insignificant and minuscule to what has occurred, but this is all I can offer. Please express this apology to Lisa as well.

In closing, I can only say I stand before you my son,
guilty, but forgiven. My prayer is that you will find forgive-
ness in your heart for me.
My love always,
Mom

p.s. Please give Zachary a hug and kiss from G.G. Please
do not stop sending me pictures and letters over this.

I didn't know how to respond to Mother's letter, so in many
ways, I didn't. Since we had begun communicating by mail,
Aunt Carolyn had cautioned me to be careful of Mother's manip-
ulative manner. As I read and re-read Mother's letter, I was on
heightened alert for her statements of self-pity, making excuses,
or potential manipulation of my emotions. While I sensed a trace
of that, I had to admit, it was minimal.

More significantly, this was the first time since Dad's murder
that Mother had ever told me straight out that she had taken
responsibility for putting the wheels in motion. It was also my
first information about her perspective regarding the plea bargain offered to her.

I was impressed, too, by her spiritual confidence. Although
her resignation to being executed also came through the pages,
her assurance of going to heaven was comforting in some measure. Her phrase, "Guilty, but forgiven" resonated with me, as
well. Weren't we all? It was only the mercy and grace of God
that gave any of us the audacity to think that we would be wor-
thy of going to heaven.

Mother's closing prayer, "that you will find forgiveness in
your heart for me," also stirred me. This was her first tenuous
probe into my heart, and I wasn't certain I liked it. Was she
reaching out to me, making overtures asking my forgiveness, or
was she subtly trying to manipulate me? The skeptic in me was

raising red flags in every direction. Yet I had been grappling with forgiveness issues for several years, now, and here it was coming to me again, not from a sermon or a song, but through words written by my own mother.

I wasn't sure whether I was ready to deal with all this, but apparently God was. He was showing me in incremental steps that I had a lot to learn about forgiveness. I thought I could forgive the people who had hurt me in my life on my own conditions, but God was showing me, "No, that is not what I said." I began to realize that although I thought I had forgiven my mother and other people in my life, I really hadn't.

CHAPTER 14

Do You Really Want
to Teach?

When Lisa and I moved to Nashville, I assumed that I could get another teaching job with relative ease. I was wrong. Not surprisingly, the best public schools were popular with parents and teachers alike, and the private schools were overloaded with qualified applicants. Exacerbating matters further, although I was working toward my teaching certification in Biology, as yet, I was certified only to teach Physical Education and to coach.

I had never really had to pursue a job in Memphis. I always had connections, friends, or other business relationships, that helped open the doors for me. When I began teaching, I went back to my old high school, and was hired almost immediately, thanks to some connections.

But when Lisa and I moved to Nashville, we didn't really know anyone who could help me get my foot in the door at a job opportunity. Lisa got a job working for a publishing company, but I could not get hired for a teaching position.

After a few miserable years of working in the automotive industry, God put into motion something totally unexpected. My father-in-law took a position with a national private corrections management company, and knowing that I wanted to get back into teaching, he called me. "Stephen, I know you want to teach. But how badly do you want to teach? What about in prison? I have a teaching position available in one of our detention centers here in Nashville."

"Okay, I'll take it," I told him, with barely a moment of hesitation.

I was not nervous about the job until the first day I walked into the prison. Hearing the cell doors clank shut behind me was an unsettling feeling, knowing that I was locked in with a large number of convicted criminals. Safety was a very real concern. Of course, it was impossible not to think that my own mother was incarcerated in a prison, as well. My only images of prison were what I had seen on television, and I quickly learned that the Hollywood renditions of prison life were far from reality. It was not chaotic or disruptive. For the most part, it was quite orderly, with only occasional flare ups.

I sat in a room with twenty-four or more inmates, three or four times a day, in close quarters. Since it was a lower security facility, most of the inmates in my classes had been convicted of crimes such as drug offenses or simple assault. I wanted to be a positive influence, so I determined that I would show the inmates respect, whether other people did or not. When a new class came in, I leveled with them. "Look, you show me respect, and I will show you respect." Most of the inmates responded quite positively to my approach.

Teaching in the prison, I noticed two things rather quickly: one, there were some incredibly bright and creative people incarcerated there, people who had a lot to offer; and two, many of the people in prison were not much different from me, except that their sins, mistakes, and crimes had been found out and were being punished in a more obvious way.

I taught basic business communication skills as well as a computer skills classes. After teaching in prison for about six months or so, I realized, *God has me here for a reason, and it is not simply to teach.*

Strange as it might seem, prior to Lisa's and my move to Nashville, I rarely thought about my mother's whereabouts. Of course, I knew that she was incarcerated, and I'd heard that the prison was located somewhere outside Nashville. Now, through an ironic set of twists and turns, God had brought me to Nashville, and here I was teaching in—of all places—a prison. Unconsciously, I was learning more of what my mother was experiencing on a daily basis. I was teaching in a relatively "safe" environment. She was incarcerated in a maximum security prison on death row. I never told any of the inmates that I had a relative in prison, but it definitely gave me an increased empathy for them, since I knew the prison experience from the other side of the visitors' room. I knew what it felt like to be on the outside looking in. I knew what it meant to live with the ramifications of someone's crime. Again, although I couldn't really see it at the time—or maybe I simply didn't want to—God was setting me up. He was getting me accustomed to prison life, educating me in ways He knew would come in handy in the years ahead.

Because of my own faith in Jesus Christ, I looked for opportunities to share the love of God with the inmates in my classes without overstepping my boundaries as a teacher. Although there were faith-based programs ministering within the prison, as a state prison employee, I was restricted regarding what I could say about my own faith in God.

Near the end of my tenure there, I dismissed class one day, and as the other inmates filed out of the room, one man lingered, obviously intending to stay behind. I was immediately on alert, since it was against protocol for an inmate to stay after class, and I knew the man could get into trouble by disobeying the rules.

He approached me and spoke quietly to me. "Something's different about you," he said. "What is it that's so different about you?"

Because he had opened the door, I could freely share with him about my faith in Jesus Christ, so I briefly told him.

He looked back at me and said, "I hope I can get to where you are." He quickly slipped out of the room, and I never had another opportunity to talk with him personally. But his words were an encouragement to me.

I taught in the prison for a full year and learned far more than I taught. God was getting me ready for something else.

When a teaching position became available at a Christian school, I took it, even though we lived about forty-five minutes south of the school. The following year I also went back to college to work on my master's degree at Middle Tennessee State University, about forty-five minutes east of our home. Consequently, I was driving for more than two hours every school day and more on the two nights a week I was in class at the university. It was a crazy schedule, but I was glad to do it because I was back in the classroom.

Throughout this time, the communication between Mother, Lisa, and I continued. Although we wrote back and forth freely, we did not discuss anything that had happened in the past. Most of our letters remained on a surface level, including some basic information about family members, and of course, the latest details about our baby boy. Mom always seemed excited to hear news of Zachary.

Neither Lisa nor I asked questions about Mom's prison life or any of her activities or routines. Occasionally, Mom might mention something about life "inside," but we never delved further into her statements. In some ways, perhaps, I didn't want to know what she was experiencing in prison—or worse yet, I didn't care. Reading letters from Mother tended to bring everything back to me, triggering unpleasant memories that I had tried to forget.

Lisa was much better about writing to Mom than I was. Sometimes she'd ask me, "Do you want to write to your mom?"

"No, I'm too tired," I might say. "I don't really have anything to say."

"Well, do you care if I write to her?"

"That's fine with me," I responded indifferently.

Lisa's compassion for my mother was amazing. She didn't feel compelled to write, but she wanted Mother to know about her grandchild and some of what was going on in my life. Mother usually wrote back letters addressed to both of us, even if Lisa was the only one writing to her. She never asked us for anything in her letters, although she emphasized how much the pictures of Zachary meant to her.

It wasn't really a conscious decision, but Lisa picked up on Mom's desire to see her grandchild. "Are you okay with me sending your mom pictures of Zachary?" Lisa asked.

"Okay, fine," I replied reticently.

Occasionally, Mother might include some statements in her letters that indicated she had renewed her faith in Jesus Christ. As she put it, "I've come full circle." It was clear that in some ways, even though she had been a religious person who faithfully attended church services, Mom felt that it was not until going to prison that she really established her own relationship with the Lord for the first time.

Often, even when I did write to Mother, I might start a letter and write a few paragraphs and then I'd turn the letter over to

Lisa to complete. In retrospect, I had a bit of the "older brother's attitude" toward the prodigal son. I was glad Mother was back with the Father, but I was not going to go out of my way to celebrate with her.

Besides her letters, she sent cards for birthdays and holidays, and always sent along special gifts for all of us at Christmas and on our birthdays. I didn't ask how long it took to earn enough money to buy those presents, working at a wage of around eleven cents an hour. Nor did I ask who "on the outside" was purchasing the presents on Mom's behalf. I guessed that was part of the service prison volunteers provided for the inmates, but I really didn't know.

Every so often, Mother alluded to Dad's death. Shortly after Christmas, she wrote, "One of my friends here heard from her son for the first time in fifteen years on Christmas Eve by way of a card. I knew exactly how she felt when I heard from you and Lisa on Christmas Eve 2001. Nothing like it. I pray that I will eventually hear from Brian again. I love you boys so much and know I have brought so much pain to you, but I never ever intended to. If I could change anything, you have to know I would."

Lisa wrote to Mom more frequently and in greater detail than I did, but I tried to send along an encouraging word here and there. As time went by, Mom became a little more open in talking about the day-to day existence in prison. At one point, she asked us to pray for the women in the facility. "As you pray," Mother wrote, "please pray for the women here. There is a lot of pain and I know you may not understand this. I just ask that you remember the women here. We have some who are still juveniles and I guess the oldest is about seventy-four."

About the time Zachary was a toddler, another attorney, Gretchen Swift, came to our house. At the time, Gretchen worked in the federal public defenders' office, but she was not working directly with Mother's case. She had visited with Mother in prison, though, and the two women had struck up a friendship. Gretchen was a young, unmarried woman when she first met Mother, and she had no idea of all the previous troubles we had encountered with other public defenders. She had discovered we lived one street over from the church she was attending and innocently thought it would be okay to walk up and talk with us. She had some gifts from Mother for Zachary and wanted to deliver them, and she had hoped to take some photographs back to Mother in prison.

I didn't know this attorney, and frankly, I was not about to let somebody I didn't know take pictures of our son. The incident irritated me, and although I didn't berate Mother again because of another lawyer showing up uninvited, the event put me off enough that writing to her seemed a lower priority. In truth, both Lisa and I were extremely busy. Regardless, we went several months without writing to Mother at all.

Mother sent several letters to us within that same time period, the worry and exasperation more evident in each one. Finally, she made the connection between our pull back in communication and Gretchen Swift's visit. Mother wrote:

> I am concerned since I have not heard from you since September. I asked once before that if I said anything or did anything that offended you, would you tell me, and you assured me that you would.
>
> I know you stay very busy. But it's just been so long since hearing from you and seeing how big Zachary has gotten. I hope Zachary received his birthday books and toy and his Christmas sweater. It's not about thank you . . . just to know he got them.

Mother then launched into an apology for Gretchen's visit:

Stephen and Lisa, if mine and Gretchen's idea of her bringing Zachary his birthday present offended you in any way, I sincerely apologize. Gretchen suggested this and I thought it sounded so neat. But it may not have sounded that way to you. If not, I am sorry and will never do anything like this again. Gretchen is such a beautiful Christian. She loves children (baby-sits for her friends who have children) and she would have liked to have met you. Every time she has visited since October, the first thing she asks is if I have heard from you. She's concerned that her desire to deliver Zachary's gifts has brought a wedge between us. I have assured [her] it hasn't. I have explained that you are very busy. But after this length of time, I don't know anymore. Please forgive me if this was offensive. I never intended it to be. That was why I wrote you ahead of time telling you who she was and that she had no ulterior motive. While she is an attorney, as I told you, she is not on my case.

I won't go on and on but pray I will hear from you soon and will receive lots of photos from birthday, Christmas or anything.

In 2003, we discovered we were pregnant again. Lisa received an early negative report from the doctor. Even prior to her first scheduled appointment, she experienced complications and hurried to the doctor's office for an ultrasound. The ultrasound revealed results very similar to what she had seen when she had miscarried a few years earlier. In fact, the doctor told Lisa, "It looks as though you are already in the early stages of a miscarriage." Lisa was upset and didn't want to accept that report, but had to admit that the characteristics looked all too similar to what she had experienced previously when she miscarried.

"In a couple of weeks," the doctor suggested, "if you are in a store, you might want to pick up a home pregnancy test, just to check to see if you are still pregnant."

Lisa recoiled at that idea. *No way am I going to do that,* she thought. She went home and totally redid our bathroom—by herself! Pouring herself into work on the remodeling project was Lisa's way of coping with the negative news.

But a few weeks later, she was walking down an aisle in a store and spotted a pregnancy test. "Okay, why not?"

She purchased the test and went home. Sure enough, it showed positively.

She went back to the doctor and they did another ultrasound. The results were conclusive: Growing within Lisa was another baby.

Early on, Lisa was nauseated quite frequently, and her pregnancy was not an easy time for us. Nevertheless, our second son, Joshua Dean, was born without complications on March 19, 2004. We were thrilled, and caring for Zachary and our newborn son, Joshua, took precedence over any thoughts or concerns we had about my mom.

A few months later, we moved again. The move had been totally unplanned, but I had been scanning the Internet one evening, when we found a house we liked. We called our realtor, went and saw the house on a Sunday, signed a contract on the house on Tuesday, put our home up for sale on Wednesday, sold our home on Thursday, and moved two weeks later at the end of June! It was a whirlwind of activity, but the new house was just what we wanted. Our lives were busy beyond anything we imagined. Lisa was caring for two young boys, while still working two days each week, and I was going to school at nights working on my master's degree, and beginning yet another teaching and coaching job. We were nonetheless ecstatic.

I wrote to Mother in March 2004 informing her of Joshua's birth, but apparently she had not received my letter. So when I responded to her, in addition to conveying the usual smattering of family information, my goal was twofold; one, to allay her concerns that something was wrong, and two, to let her know that I was not pleased by the attorney's visit. I let Mother know both rather brusquely.

"There is nothing wrong," I began. "Actually we wrote a letter and sent some pictures to you. Obviously, you did not receive the letter. The pictures were of all of us, including Joshua Dean, the newest addition to the family. I sent that letter right after we got settled from being in the hospital (around the end of March)." I went on to inform Mother that I would be changing jobs again and that I would be graduating with my masters degree in August. "I think Lisa is happy," I wrote, "because for the first time in many years, I will not be going to college." Then I got to the point of my letter.

> As far as the situation with Gretchen, I cannot imagine the feelings that you have to deal with. However, I have to feel like I am protecting my family. Her coming by is not acceptable. I appreciate the gifts that you send. But, the way that you have sent them in the past is effective. I would prefer to leave it that way. She may be a great person, however, I am not comfortable with people showing up and wanting to take pictures of my family. I have and will do my best to continue sending pictures. I know that they mean a lot to you. I will not quit sending them for stupid reasons.

I then felt that I needed to address an issue that could easily cause the thin ice of our communications to crack. I was quite blunt with Mother and stated my feelings straightforwardly.

> Mom, I am thirty-one years old. I know that many years have passed since you have seen me. So I can imagine how

hard it is to comprehend that on many levels. However, the truth is I am an adult and I am old enough that if I have a problem, I will let you know. I have no problems with communicating that to you. Unfortunately, you did not receive the letter I had already sent you addressing this issue. So as far as I am concerned, this is not an issue that is causing any lack of communication. I just ask that you respect my view on this type of situation.

I then made what I considered as major concessions to my mother:

I want you to realize that I love you very much. Nobody will or could ever take your place. But reality finds us in a very difficult situation. I feel that we have made tremendous strides in making this situation positive. Sometime down the road, additional steps might be a possibility. I would not tell you this if I did not mean it. However, right now my focus is on my immediate family, and me being the best husband and parent I can be. You know how difficult that task is day to day. I have no intentions of cutting off communications. There is no reason to do that. So I do not want you to be concerned with that being an issue. Whether you are physically here or not, you are still the grandmother of my children. I want to try to make them as much a part of your life as I can.

I almost surprised myself, putting on paper the words and phrases that I could hardly understand myself. In fact, I probably wasn't certain, at the time, what I meant when I implied that down the road sometime, our circumstances might change and "additional steps," whatever that might entail, might be a possibility. Looking back, I can only assume that again, God was preconditioning me to think in terms of being totally reconciled with my mother.

Maybe so, but at that moment, such a possibility still seemed like quite a pipe dream.

At the end of the 2004 academic year, the headmaster at the school where I was teaching gave me a glowing report. "I'm happy to have you here," she said, "but I realize how far you must drive each day, and the toll your schedule is taking on you and your family time." She said she knew of a headmaster who had an upcoming opening at a school closer to my home, and that she would be willing to call to see if the position had yet been filled. What she didn't know was that I had applied at that same school when we first moved to Nashville, but they weren't hiring anyone in my position.

Nevertheless, she made the call, I applied, and sure enough, the headmaster of Christ Presbyterian Academy, Richard Anderson, granted me an interview.

There was an assistant basketball coaching job coming available that they had not yet even advertised. The high school principal, Philip Boeing, hired me to teach science, to coach basketball, and to help as an assistant baseball coach, too.

Ironically, the principal who hired me retired over that summer and wasn't even there the first day of teachers' orientation meetings when I showed up for work. I didn't know a soul there and none of my coworkers knew my family background or anything about me.

Or so I thought.

CHAPTER 15

Blown Away

God was putting obvious signposts in front of me that I could not ignore, and many of those indicators were pointing toward the Tennessee Prison for Women.

I knew that something was changing within me, and I recognized that it was God-driven. I realized that I was making progress in the area of forgiveness because I no longer got angry at Mother anymore every time I thought of Dad. I still became emotional at times, and cringed at the missed opportunities to have my parents as part of my life, and now, as part of the lives of Lisa and my children. But the bitterness had begun to dissipate. Slowly, I was coming to the place where it no longer mattered who did what in Mom's and Dad's relationship; the simple truth was that I didn't have a father or a mother in my life, and I was still longing for that parental influence. I realized that I could either deal with it and move on, or else it would overwhelm me.

That was the message God was burning into my heart, so naturally, when I was asked to give a testimony to the freshman Bible class, during my first year at my new school, that was the thrust of the message I shared with the students. As I sat in the classroom, I shared my story of how Mother had instigated the murder of my dad. The students listened intently, practically mesmerized; this was obviously a whole new world for them. This wasn't a movie in a theater or a song on the radio. This was a real person, a teacher, telling them that horrible wrongs can occur—did occur—and can color our lives forever if we allow them to do so.

I closed by saying, "We've all gone through some stuff. We've all been hurt in some way; all of our spirits have been wounded." I looked around the room into the eyes of the young students watching and listening to me. Even as high school freshmen— perhaps especially as high school freshmen—they understood the pain of being wounded by someone they loved.

But I didn't want them to stop there. "God gives you an opportunity to get up and move on," I said, "or you can go through life feeling as though people owe you something all the time. God gives you the strength to get up and move on. You don't have the right to sit around and wallow in despair. God will bless you if you get up and move on."

Afterwards, Steve Wilson, one of the faculty members in the classroom that day, stopped me in the hall. I didn't really know Steve, but he looked intently at me.

Steve said, "You're Stephen Owens?"

"Yeah . . ."

"And Gaile Owens is your mother?"

"Yes," I said tentatively, wondering where this was going.

"I think I have been ministering to your mother in my prison ministry."

"You what?"

Steve smiled. "Some friends and I have volunteered at the prison for years. We do some Bible studies, and I lead in some worship music in the prison chapel, and even do a little preaching now and then. I think your mom has been coming to our services for a long time. If it is her, she's actually one of the spiritual leaders in the prison. She's a great influence, especially on some of the younger inmates who are coming in scared, sometimes hostile, and carrying a lot of baggage. She helps with baptismal services, and everything."

I was blown away by what Steve told me. We talked briefly and then headed on to our next classes, but I could not shake his words from my mind. Over the next weeks and months, Steve and I grew to be good friends, as well as colleagues.

"You really need to come with me sometime," he offered one day when we were talking.

"Come where?" I asked naively.

"To the prison," he said, as casually as though he were talking about going to a ballgame. "I know your mom would love to see you. She'd probably never ask you, but if you ever want to visit her, I'll be glad to help."

"Ahh, no, thank you, man," I said, my mind stumbling to find the right words. I shook my head. "I don't think I'm quite ready for that yet." I took a deep breath. "Maybe someday."

Steve looked at me and nodded. "Okay, just let me know. I've been going out there for a long time. The guards and the warden know me. I'll be glad to help facilitate a visit, whenever you'd like."

"Thanks, Steve. I appreciate your concern," I said honestly. What I didn't say was probably equally as true: that I had no intention of going to that prison. It would take an act of God to get me to visit my mother in that prison.

Steve Wilson informed Mother about my talk to the freshmen, as well as what he perceived as my openness to the possibility of visiting her in prison sometime. She seized on that idea, and in short order, Steve brought me some papers to complete, required for visitation at the Tennessee Prison for Women. I quickly set the papers aside. Along with her presumption about visitation, I sensed a bit of "whining" on Mother's part because we had not recently written or sent photos of Joshua and Zachary, so I decided to nip it in the bud.

> *In a previous note from you, you had mentioned the conversation with Steve Wilson and the papers to visit. To be honest, I just haven't taken the time to fill them out. Also, as you can, I hope, understand, there is still some [discomfort] in visiting you in that environment. Plus the fact that we have not met face to face in almost twenty years. That is not really due to a fault of yours or mine. I feel it has just been a growing up of a young man. I feel God put me in the prison I taught in for a year to prepare me for this day . . . I believe that God has gotten me to this place for a reason . . . I know that you miss not being able to see the grandchildren, however, I feel that gives some idea of how I have felt for years not being able to have the privilege of you nor Dad around to experience my accomplishments and defeats. Plus especially being able to see the joy I feel that both of you would have experienced with my children. Even twenty years later, I often wonder what that experience would have been like. This is not an attempt to make you feel worse than you already do; it is a grown man expressing his feelings, now that I am at a place to do that.*

From August 2005 to January 2008, Lisa and I rarely wrote to Mother. It wasn't negligence; nor were we intentionally snubbing her. Our lives simply got incredibly busy. Between changing jobs, teaching new subject material, coaching, and trying to help Lisa with the boys, I had little spare time for writing letters. That was my excuse, anyhow, and it was a convenient rationalization when I thought of Mother. It worked well with everybody except God.

Mother, of course, was frantic. On December 22, 2007, she wrote:

> *Dear Stephen and Lisa,*
>
> *I hope this letter finds you all doing good. I had prayed I would hear from you before Christmas as it is now two years since I received a photo or heard from you. I have cried, prayed, cried, and prayed, wondering what I said or didn't say that caused you not to communicate even minimally with me. I quit writing and begging for photos thinking maybe this is what I was supposed to do.*
>
> *I keep going back to the letter you wrote me Stephen where you addressed my not being there for your accomplishments and your failures. There's nothing I regret any more than this, however, as I have tried to know what was going on in your life, you continued to not answer questions, much less my letters . . . Stephen, I don't know why after all this time you stopped writing and sending photos. But this has been one of the most painful things for me for the past two years. I can only see the [children] grow through photos, as I did you and Brian. I know it's not your fault and I am not saying that. I just beg you to allow me to see them through photos. I haven't and I will never ask you to bring them to this place. That will have to be your decision. To be honest, things are such that my appeal process is nearing an end and I have not had your or Brian's name on any of my files here, so if my sentence is carried out, I am hoping you will be protected. I can't guarantee anything, but I have for years done everything I could to protect you and Brian. I know at times it has not worked but I have tried.*

My last appeal will be heard in Cincinnati at the 6th circuit court on January 29. It had been scheduled for December 4, but one of my attorneys had a death in the family. This is the last appeal I will file. I am not going to go through all the media circus of last minute appeals, etc. Twenty-two years is enough. So this may or may not be my last Christmas, only God knows.

If Mother thought that the oft-used "threat" foisted on families by self-pitying parents and grandparents for generations—"I may not be here next year this time"—would stimulate letters from me, she was wrong. Although I didn't want to be mean to Mom, neither was she at the top of my priority list. For me, my wife and children and my responsibilities at work came first. Unfortunately, by the time I completed all that I wanted to do at home, there was little time left over for writing letters. Looking back, I see now that I probably had no driving desire to write, either. Even her request for more pictures of Zachary and Joshua went unattended.

Mom wrote a similar letter on June 1, 2008.

Stephen, I am writing this letter to ask that you please allow me to see the boys grow up through photos. I don't know why you no longer write, but I have to respect your decision. I haven't asked anything of either of you boys. Photos were all I had as the two of you grew into the fine young men you are today. I'll be honest, those photos that Thelma assured I received are what kept me going. Don't get me wrong, the photos were bitter sweet, but at least I could see you growing up. This is all I am asking of you related to Zachary and Joshua. Is this too much to ask? I have not seen photos in over two years now, and I know the boys are so big and have changed.

*As the time frame grew from months to years of not
hearing from you, I decided to not write, as I didn't know
if you wanted to hear from me or not. I have tried all
these years to do whatever I knew or thought that you boys
wanted. When Carolyn would say that to talk to me was
upsetting to you boys, I quit calling. I would write and send
surprises periodically, but never knew if you got them or not.
I never knew exactly what to do. I respected Carolyn's wishes
to not call, etc. as I had to believe this is what you boys
wanted. But I never knew. I dreamed of the day I would
see you two boys again, but this never happened and I am
not expecting it to happen now. My love is still the same; I
couldn't love you boys more. I don't know much about your
lives as you have chosen not to share it with me, but nothing
will ever take my love for you.*

*I wish I could go back and change things, but I can't.
While I know God has forgiven me and I try to forgive
myself, I am constantly tormented by the things that have
happened. Wishing for all of our lives to be different.
Wishing for hugs from you boys, etc. None of which I will
ever have.*

*Stephen, I don't want you to take the things I have said
as some form of manipulation. I just want you to know that
I have not lived a day without pain and regret. Whether you
can understand this or not, I love and will always love your
dad. If I could change anything for you, I promise you, I
would.*

Whether it was pity, sorrow, guilt, or God's leading, Mother's
plaintive cry through her June letter prompted a response from
me—the first letter I returned to her in more than two and a
half years. I straightforwardly admitted to her that there was no
real reason I had not written.

I want to apologize for not writing. There really isn't any reason that I haven't other than I just get wrapped up in my everyday things to do. Lisa is always on me about returning letters to you. I have gone as far as typing a few, but not printing or mailing them, just because of my constant busy schedule, and honestly, not taking the time to do it. That is not a good reason, but it is the reason you have not heard from me.

I shared some news about the kids and even included a few photos. I then felt it important to address some of the subtle implications in Mother's letter, especially her notion that Brian and I did not want to hear from her during our childhood. "Aunt Carolyn's remarks about hearing from you were appropriate early on as we were younger. I think we were still trying to find our own place, as we worked through everything."

I then delivered what I was certain would be a bombshell in Mother's heart, although I didn't say it to offer false hope, but to encourage her.

I really intend to come visit you. That is a big step for me to take, even at thirty-five years of age. I want to do this because I think it would produce the last stage of closure for me. That doesn't mean that I would only visit once. If you could have someone send me the papers to fill out to visit, I would appreciate it. If you can't, then let me know what I need to do. I have filled out the papers once a long time ago and never sent them in.

Mom, as you stated, nothing in the past could be changed. In fact, I have learned a lot through this whole process, as a man and father. That does not mean that I wouldn't have things be different or normal (whatever that is). At this point in my life, there really isn't anger or resentment. I have just tried to go on with my life and do what

*I think is best for my family. However, I wouldn't say that
there is a great closeness in the [extended] family anymore. I
think part of that is due to distance and the effects of Brian
and me really being on our own. Also, with not many relatives still alive, and no real contact with Dad's family for
years, this made the separation happen faster. I am not saying
this to make you feel bad, just being honest.*

Whether I was writing to her or not, God was continually
bringing to mind my relationship with Mother. Every once in
a while, of course, Steve Wilson reminded me about his offer
to accompany me if I ever wanted to visit Mother in prison. I
didn't. But I always thanked him sincerely for caring. Despite
consistently declining Steve's kind offer, the issue of visiting my
mother in prison continued to nag at my mind. Increasingly, I
thought, *How can I teach these kids in a Christian school about
the love of God, yet continue to harbor any resentment toward my
mother?* God had been working on me for a number of years, so
I no longer hated her. But the bitterness was much more difficult
to resolve.

CHAPTER 16

Redeemed

There have been two times in my life when I've known for certain that I had heard from God, that I knew God's hand was in this, and He was directing my paths. One of those incidents was the day Steve Wilson told me in the hallway that he had been ministering to my mom for more than ten years.

The other was in late July / early August 2008, when I was out running for exercise. As I usually did when I ran, I carried an iPod with the music filling my ears with rich, inspiring sounds and messages. That day as I was running, a song by Nicole C. Mullen, "(I Know) My Redeemer Lives," began playing in my ears. Suddenly, it was as though God was speaking through that song right into my heart and mind.

I honestly don't remember a thing from the time the song came on until I reached my home. People may have been honking at me, or waving at me as I ran, but I was totally oblivious to everything around me. I was in a "zone" with God. I remember where I was when the music came on, but I can't remember another thing about that run until I found myself in my drive-way. I don't even remember running the rest of the way. But during that time, I know beyond a doubt that God told me two clear messages: "I have you where you need to be, and you know what you need to do."

For much of my life, I had been skeptical of people who dared to declare they had heard a word from God. But without a glimmer of doubt, I know I heard from God that day.

When I snapped out of my reverie and found myself in front of our home, I knew that I could no longer ignore what God was saying to me. That very day, I initiated actions to secure the paperwork that I needed to complete to go visit my mother in prison.

That same day, during a pre-school-term orientation session at Christ Presbyterian Academy, the school where I was teach-ing, I boldly announced to the faculty and administrators that I felt God was instructing me to go visit Mom at some point. I didn't put a date on my goal, but something about stating it in public solidified the commitment in my mind.

Now just because I had made that public declaration did not mean that I ran to the prison the following week. Far from it! It was another entire year before I would fill the papers out for the initial visit. In the meantime, Steve Wilson kept nudging me toward the prison. He'd bring me another edition of visitation forms to fill out and I would lay them aside or throw them away. I sensed that God was leading me to visit Mom, but I just wasn't ready to go. I realized that although God may lead a person to do something, He still allows us an astounding measure of free will in making those decisions.

My reluctance to fill out the paperwork to go see Mom was similar to the Old Testament prophet Jonah's reluctance when God instructed him to go to Nineveh and preach a message of salvation. Jonah knew very well where God had told him to go and what God wanted him to do; Jonah just didn't want to go. We know what happened to him, being cast overboard during a storm, then swallowed by a large fish, probably some sort of whale, and then spewed up onto the shore—where God gave Jonah fresh instruction to go to Nineveh, right where he didn't want to go.

By 2008, God had taken away the anger from my heart. And my reluctance to visit my mother wasn't based in rebellion against God's instructions. What I was fighting within was the nervousness and the uncertainty of the unknown. What would it really be like to see Mother again? Although I never questioned that I had heard from God, I still had moments when I wondered, "God, is this really you or is this all in my own imagination?"

The issue became more focused in late August 2008 when I received a letter from attorney Gretchen Swift, who was now handling Mom's case directly. Gretchen wrote:

> *I am writing to you because I, along with my co-counsel Kelley Henry, represent Gaile Owens in federal court proceedings. I made contact with you several years ago—around your son's birthday or perhaps Christmas—in order to deliver gifts to your son from Ms. Owens. I believe that at that point, you were not interested in speaking with me. I have tried to respect your privacy since then, and I do understand the importance of maintaining that privacy for you and your family and the very difficult and painful circumstance that you are in because of Ms. Owens's case. However, I am contacting you now because Ms. Owens's case has reached a critical point, and my co-counsel and I were hoping to have the opportunity to meet with you to discuss what is happening in her case and offer our assistance to you in the future.*
>
> *We stopped by your home yesterday evening hoping to meet with you. Our intention was not to scare you or offend*

*you or anyone else—we certainly hope that we didn't. While
we do want to respect your privacy and the privacy of your
family, we do believe that at this point in Ms. Owens's case, it
is important for you and Ms. Owens that we have the chance
to talk with you. As I stated, Ms. Owens's case has reached
a critical point. Her case has advanced into the appellate
courts—we are currently awaiting a decision from the Sixth
Circuit Court of Appeals. After the Court's decision, the
next step would be to proceed to the United Stated Supreme
Court, and then into clemency.*

The subtle implication of the lawyer's letter was not lost on
me: unless something extraordinary occurred, Mother's days
were numbered. She was running out of legal options, and by
the lawyer even mentioning the future possibilities, it said to me
that the odds indicated Mother was going to lose.

Throughout late 2008 and the spring of 2009, there were several more times when I started filling out the visitation request
forms, and then stopped short; I wouldn't complete them, or
wouldn't send them. Lisa didn't push me about the visitation.
Earlier in our marriage, she'd sometimes ask me, "Do you want
to go see your mom in prison?"

My response was consistently the same. "No, I'm really not
interested in doing that."

But after Zachary was born, things changed, my answer
wasn't quite as rigid. "I've thought about it," I replied when Lisa
asked about visiting my mother, "but I don't know if I am ready
yet." Still, Lisa didn't push.

As the boys grew older, they questioned Lisa and me more
frequently and more specifically about their grandparents. We
knew the day was coming when they would want more information than we were currently giving them. But how much should
we tell them, when, and how? We refused to lie to our kids, yet
we didn't know how much information was age appropriate for

them. Lisa and I grappled with those questions more and more. We realized that we needed some outside help, so we set up an appointment with a pastoral counselor at our church.

Zachary, in particular, was putting the pieces of the puzzle together. He zeroed in on the issue that he never saw any grandparents from my side of the family. Occasionally, he asked me about my parents. "We see Mommy's mom and dad, but we never see your mom or dad."

I placated him with answers such as, "Well, Zachary, I have a mom and dad just like you."

For a long time, that was sufficient. Increasingly, though, Zachary turned back to the question, either to me or to Lisa, "Where's Daddy's mom and dad? We know your mom and dad, but we never see Daddy's mom and dad." At some point along the way, we even informed him that my dad had passed away when I was a little boy. But we knew there were some things that he wasn't yet old enough to be told.

One night in the spring of 2009, less than two weeks after Lisa and I had sought help from the spiritual counselor, she and I were lying in bed talking when Zachary came into our bedroom. He had already been asleep, but something had awakened him, so he came to our room. Zachary purposely avoided my side of the bed and eased to the side closest to Lisa. "I have to talk to Mom," he said.

"Mom," he said, "Where is Dad's mom?" Zachary asked Lisa.

The moment I heard our son's question, I choked up. I couldn't say a word, as I struggled to fight back the tears. Lisa looked at me and saw the tears already streaming down my face.

"Zachary, sit right here," Lisa responded, patting the bed. "Let's talk about this." She carefully explained that my dad had passed away, and my mom, Granny Gaile, was in prison. "We need to pray for G.G., Daddy's mom."

"When will she get out? Will she ever get out and come see us?"

"We hope so. That's one of the things we just have to pray about," Lisa replied. "God knows." She and Zachary talked further and Lisa provided him as much information as she felt appropriate for his age and understanding. Meanwhile, I was an emotional mess. When the conversation concluded, I got it together well enough to reaffirm what Lisa was telling him. Zachary stepped to the foot of the bed, and asked, "Are you okay, Dad?"

I wiped the tears from my eyes and swallowed hard. "Yes, Zachary, I'm okay," I answered. "Zachary, I love you, son. And Mom and Dad will tell you more when you need to know more. Right now, you just have to trust Mom and Dad, okay?"

"Yes, sir," he said, and went on back to bed. I realized that the boys had real questions and I desperately wanted to do the right thing in trying to let them know what was going on without striking fear in their hearts, or prejudicing them against their grandmother.

Interestingly, the boys didn't know that Lisa and I had previously seen a counselor, seeking help in how to tell them about their paternal grandparents. But God knew we needed to get ready, so He provided the extra wisdom at just the right time.

In some of Mom's letters she indicated that she had sought and received forgiveness from God for her past sins. Although she didn't say so directly, I had to assume that included her sins against Dad.

For many years, I really didn't know how Mom was faring in prison, what her health and mental state were, what sort of experiences she might be enduring, or what her chances were of living another day—nor did I care.

While living in Memphis, I had never really investigated any of the court documents concerning Mom's case. Now that we lived in Nashville, and I considered going to visit my mother, as difficult as it might be, I felt it important to at least peruse the court documents. They weren't hard to find. Most of the pertinent information regarding the crime, the court case, and appeals was readily available online.

When Lisa and I first read the court documents describing both Mom's and Dad's actions, we were shocked. The court proceedings were a sham, replete with ineptitude and legal missteps. Examining the court documents raised as many questions for me as answers. Looking at the intimate details about Mom's and Dad's relationship and the events that led to Dad's murder was gut-wrenching for me. Worse yet, it was impossible to determine who was telling the truth.

As Lisa and I discussed Mother's case, Lisa reminded me, "You're going to have to accept the fact that you may never get absolute answers this side of heaven. You're going to have to decide, based solely on what you believe God wants you to do, because there is a strong possibility that you may never know what actually happened."

As I went back and looked at the accusations, even though I had never witnessed anything out of the ordinary, I had to admit that there must have been something askew in Mom's and Dad's marriage. The difficulty, of course, was trying to figure out the truth in what was basically a "he-said; she-said" situation, and Dad was not here to defend himself. Still, whether Dad did the things Mom told her attorneys and counselors that he did or not, there must have been something that drove her to such a radical response.

Many nights as Lisa and I wrestled with the information, trying to determine what was true or false, I simply had to walk away from it. I'd get so frustrated as I tried to sort through it all and grapple in my mind with the ramifications, I couldn't take it any more.

"We're done," I'd say. I wasn't angry with Lisa; I simply couldn't take any more of the awful details of my family history. For years because I had focused so much on the brutality of what had happened, I regarded Dad as an angel and Mom as on her way to hell. Now as we sifted through the court documents, I had to face the fact that my dad was not a perfect man, and that he had more flaws than I cared to admit. Dealing with my disappointment about Dad was difficult.

God finally brought me to a point where it no longer mattered who was right or wrong. I didn't worry about it. The question was not which person was more wrong than the other, Mother or Dad; the question was: Would I obey God and do what He was asking me to do?

Whether it was a mother-son connection, healing in my own heart and mind, or God at work in all of us, I slowly lowered the barriers. I couldn't see far down the road, or even where these inclinations were taking me, but as best I could, I tried to do whatever God put in front of me. I had no pre-planned course of action; each tenuous step of obedience was one more in which God was guiding me, directing me, molding me.

When I decided that I wanted to examine the documents and see for myself, I discovered information about the letters that Dad had written to another woman who worked at the hospital with whom he was having an affair. I read about a letter that had been in his desk drawer, written to Dad from that same woman.

Not only did I have to forgive Mom, but as I pored over court documents and learned more about my father's faults, I confronted tangible reports that my dad wasn't perfect, either. I realized I had to forgive my dad, as well.

Tired of feeling the heavy burden of unforgiveness, weary of carrying the weight on my shoulders, I was miserable, even on my better days, because I knew that I hadn't dealt well with the matters of forgiveness and reconciliation. Slowly, almost imperceptibly, I moved to the point where it no longer mattered whether I could prove what my mother said or what my father might have done. All that mattered was that I forgive them both.

CHAPTER 17

The Blog

For most of the tumultuous spiritual journey on which I was traveling, my closest companion was my wife Lisa. She believed in me, and often encouraged me to tell my story to others, but being a private sort of person, I usually found some reason to remain quiet about my past. My restraint did not stem from bashfulness or a fear of talking in public. It wasn't that I couldn't talk about it, but for years, I simply didn't want to say any more about the experiences that had so indelibly shaped my life. Lisa reminded me occasionally that the events through which we had worked—and were still working—might be helpful to others. Beyond that, we intensely felt the need of prayer support as we engaged in the spiritual battles surrounding this newfound relationship with my mother. So rather than trying to communicate with all our friends and family members by phone, letter, or e-mail, I decided to put my thoughts into a blog and upload it online.

I called my blog "He Will Deliver" and titled my first attempt at blogging, "I Give In" on February 9, 2009, a little more than a week before the twenty-fourth anniversary of finding my dad on the floor of our den. I began straightforwardly:

No excuses. This blog is my passive response to God's persistent voice. I've tried to ignore Him. I've tried to take baby steps to quiet the voice and then move on with my day. So here I am now. My only expectation is to put myself out there. God will take care of the rest . . . Do I think God created the tragedy when I was 12 years old? No. I think what happened to my family was evil. Of course I still struggle. Of course I still get furious about it. My heart aches with pain so great I have to remind myself to breathe. But living through a tragedy does not entitle me to an easy life. I believe innocent families suffer through horrible events every day. I am aware that others have suffered through much more.

But I cannot shake God's voice to share my story and walk out loud through my ongoing journey. So, I will consent and obey. I feel His guidance and His direction and I know He will deliver.

I didn't write another blog entry for six months. Nor did I make much progress in executing the paperwork required to visit Mother. Neither example of restraint was due to unwillingness, oversight, or negligence. Time just slipped away from me.

I had stood before the faculty and staff at school in August of 2008, had given my testimony and announced the decision that God had placed on my heart—that I knew it was time to visit my mother in prison, and I was ready to move forward. Lisa and I completed the paperwork, and received the necessary permissions from the prison officials, and were placed on the "approved visitors" list. All that remained was for me to write Mother and schedule a time for our visit.

But then I became busy. I was busy with school, busy with basketball, busy with our kids' schedules, too. The holidays arrived right on schedule, and everyone knows the holidays are busy times. After the holidays came basketball tournaments, and the regular basketball season. I didn't want the distraction of a prison visit to take my attention away from our team.

Before I knew it, the school year was concluding and it was final exam time. I was way too busy wrapping up the school year to think about visiting my mother on death row. Then, the day of my last exam at school, Lisa, and the boys and I left for our family vacation. After that came summer basketball camps and more family travels. Suddenly, it was nearly a year later from when I first announced my intentions to visit Mother, and I had done nothing to take that pivotal first step.

My heart was heavy and I realized that God was still patiently standing beside me with outstretched arms and ready to walk with me. I also recognized that I had to be willing to ask for the help and prayers of other people. I read a Scripture verse from Exodus 23:20, that said, "See, I am sending an angel ahead of you to guard you along the way and to bring you to the place I have prepared."

Indeed, God had been preparing the way. Over the years, occasionally I reiterated to Lisa, "Someday, I probably want to see my mother again." Lisa had always encouraged me, without pressuring me. But now, Lisa reminded me, "If you hear God speaking to you, if you know in your heart that you are ready for this, then you cannot deny God the opportunity to use you. You can do this."

So as part of my preparation, I set about blogging once again. On Tuesday, July 21, 2009, my mind was racing as I reviewed some of the details with my blog readers, revealing why I so desperately requested their prayers. I uploaded this message:

> The letter to my mother, Gaile Owens, will be mailed tomorrow requesting a visit on August 23, 2009. The last time I saw my mother was in 1986 and I was sitting on the witness stand testifying against her. She was convicted of accessory before the fact in the murder of my father and sentenced to death. It certainly seems cliché to say that it has been a difficult "journey" to this place of forgiveness . . . It has been excruciating at times. It has been full of deep valleys. I have undoubtedly hit rock bottom more than once. I have been face down in the mud and mire of many pits. But I believe with all my heart that God has rescued me, carried me, led me, and has freed me. He is my Deliverer. He is my Redeemer. I still ache with pain at the loss of my father. I do not believe that ache will ever leave me. It isn't fair. But as hard as it is to understand, I still hold strong to the unfailing truth that "in ALL things God works for the good of those that love Him and are called according to His purpose." He does not only use the nicely wrapped events in life, but "ALL things" in life. This means He uses the good and the bad. He even uses the horrific and the tragic.

The following day, before I put the letter requesting the visit with Mother in the mail, I added the additional information in my blog:

> Dropping that letter in the mailbox is a HUGE step. It is not the first letter I have ever sent to my mother. Obviously, it isn't about the tangible piece of paper. It is all about what that paper represents. That letter represents forgiveness in a very raw form. After years of feeling angry, resentful, hurt, abandoned, lost, and betrayed,

I am free. That freedom has also made me feel very
exposed. As those feelings of vulnerability begin to rise
within me, I keep going back to Proverbs 3:5–6. "Trust
in the LORD with all your heart and lean not on your own
understanding. In all your ways acknowledge Him and He
will direct your paths." It is true. He has led me to this
path and He will continue to lead me. I am experiencing
the freedom of forgiveness today because 24 years ago
God directly and intentionally intervened in my life. In the
midst of evil and destruction, God wrapped His loving arms
around me and He did not leave me or forsake me. I had
my moments, days, weeks, months, and sometimes years
of doubt. I will never understand the choices made by my
mother. Why did she allow me to walk into the house that
night? Does she know that I have pictures in my head that
can never be erased? I see pictures of my father taking
his last breaths. I can still remember what I was thinking
as I approached him. I remember his clothes. I remember
my mother's reaction. How does a mother do that to her
children? I will never have the answers to my endless
questions. But as I drop that letter in the mailbox today, I
know with all my heart that God has been leading me down
this path of redemption and He is my Savior.

If I thought I would have a sense of relief at sending off the
visitation request, I was wrong. The following day, my emotions
were still bouncing all over the place. Thoughts of Dad pum-
meled my mind. Trying my best to express what I was feeling, I
attempted to blog about it:

I finally grasp the fact that I don't need answers to
forgive. Although forgiveness brings peace, it does not
erase consequences. Maybe that is an obvious realization
for many people. But for me, in this situation, it was not

so obvious. I lost both of my parents in an instant . . .
Within a few hours, my life was forever changed. I think
of my father every single day. I want him here with me. I
am often overwhelmed with sadness and grief as I think of
all that has been missed in my relationship with him. My
father didn't see me grow up. He didn't sit in the stands
in my high school games. He didn't see me graduate and
he didn't stand beside me on my wedding day. He has
not been here to teach me about fatherhood and spend
time with his grandchildren. He has missed holidays and
birthdays. After all these years I desperately long for his
physical presence in my life. The harsh reality is that my
mother has also been absent from my life. This is a healing
process. This is probably a lifelong healing process.

Unbelievable! I sent the visitation request on Wednesday, and
on Saturday, I received the same letter back in the mail, stamped,
"Return to Sender." *What's going on here?* I thought. *Is this some
kind of cruel joke? After all the years it took me to muster the courage to send that request, I now get it back in the mail? Is this Satan's
attempt to discourage me?*

When I showed the returned envelope to Lisa, she wasn't
sure whether to laugh or cry. She recognized immediately that
I had omitted Mother's Tennessee Department of Corrections
number on the address. Ordinarily, Lisa addressed most of our
cards and letters to Mother, but I wanted to handle this one
myself. I was a big boy. I could do this.

I did. And I messed up the address. We included the TDOC
number on the envelope and put the letter back in the mail. The
delay gave me another opportunity to beg my blog readers to
pray not only for me, but for my mother also, as she received the
request.

Already, Lisa and I had been receiving messages of encouragement and support from a wide assortment of people. We were

especially moved by messages from friends back in Memphis who were there for me in my time of need in the years immediately following Dad's death. I found myself actually enjoying some of their fond memories of my dad. Some of these friends had immediately stepped up in my life and had become brothers and fathers to me when I was twelve years old. These godly men, my church family, my teachers and coaches at school encircled me and would not allow me to give up. As I read their e-mails and other notes, I realized that although I felt certain that God was guiding me along the path toward expressing forgiveness to my mother, my decision to speak openly about my life and our family history might result in painful memories for others. My Aunt Carolyn, for instance, was one of the greatest influences in my life at that time, but she had been estranged from Mom for years. I didn't want to dredge up the past for her, or for my brother Brian, but I didn't know how I could avoid those memories and still do what God was leading me to do. I had to believe, though, if Jesus Christ was truly the Great Healer, as I knew Him to be, He was their Healer as well as mine.

Lisa and the boys and I traveled to Memphis to enjoy the Fourth of July celebration with Brian, his wife Staci, and their children. We had a great time, but then just as we were leaving, I received a phone call from our cousin in Arkansas. Pawpaw Owens, my dad's father, was sick and his health was declining rapidly. Our cousin implied that if we ever wanted to see him again, we should probably make a trip soon.

Lisa and I talked about my decision. Should I go see him? Would he even recognize me? I hadn't seen him in more than twenty years. In November 1984, my grandmother passed away unexpectedly from a brain aneurysm. Three months later, Dad was murdered, and my grandfather gave up on hope. He moved away and we lost all contact with him. I missed him, especially since he was one of the last connections I had with my father. Lisa and I decided that we had to go see him.

We planned a trip to Arkansas for the weekend of Friday, July 31. Just as we were leaving, the mailman brought a letter from Mom and the approved visitation request. The date for our visit was officially set for Sunday, August 23, 2009. On the approved request form was a line that had to be filled out by Mother stating the "justification for visit." Mother had written there, "first visit with son."

As I read those words, they hit me with enormous force. "First visit with son." I felt relief in finally seeing that phrase, yet overwhelmed by all that it implied.

We drove the long trip to Arkansas with our emotions already at a heightened pitch, and seeing my grandfather for the first time in more than two decades only intensified those feelings. He was obviously surprised to see us, and it felt awkward at first, but he recognized me, and before long was telling family stories. We had a good visit, and it was a blessing to me to be able to spend some time with him after all the years. On the way home, it struck me that after years of no contact, I would see both sides of the family within thirty days of each other.

On Sunday, August 2, I informed the readers of my blog that the date for my visit with Mother had been set.

> My prayers will continue to be that God's will be done. I pray for His will in the weeks leading up to August 23, for this visit with my mother on that Sunday afternoon, and for the weeks, months, and years following August 23. Right now, I don't know if this will be a one-time visit or if I will continue to schedule visits in the future. I have no expectations, but I do know that I need to look at her and tell her that I forgive her. Yes, the forgiveness exists regardless if I say it to her face. But I cannot explain the

need I have to tell her. Maybe I feel it will bring closure.
I understand it could create or recreate past feelings
of anger and pain. But I do trust God with all my heart.
I know it may not make sense. I know it is completely
understandable to never want to see her again. But I feel
deep within me that this truly is where God is leading me.

Many of the people who responded to my blogs, or stopped
me in the halls at school to tell me they were praying for me felt
a little awkward about asking me for details. More than a few
individuals said things such as, "I have so many questions about
what you are going through, but I don't want to intrude or be
rude."

I really didn't mind their questions. In fact, I felt that the
more people knew, the more specifically they could pray for us.
I was also hoping that the more people understood about our
story, the more they would be able to see God's work in my life
and draw encouragement from it. I wrote in my blog,

> The decision to share my life is an opportunity not an
> obligation. I have the opportunity to allow others to see
> how God has brought light into the darkest days, months,
> and years of my life. I don't HAVE to do this. I GET to do
> this. In Matthew 10:32–33, Jesus tells us that "whoever
> acknowledges me before men, I will also acknowledge
> him before my Father in heaven. But whoever disowns
> me before men, I will disown him before my Father in
> heaven." Matthew 5:14–15 says, "You are the light of the
> world. A city on a hill cannot be hidden. Neither do people
> light a lamp and put it under a bowl. Instead they put it on
> its stand, and it gives light to everyone in the house." If I
> continue to keep silent when I should speak, then I would
> be "hiding the light". Silence is no longer an option for me.

As I reflected on our visit with Dad's remaining family in Arkansas, it struck me that I was only one year younger than my dad was when he died. It was an uncomfortable thought, and one on which I didn't dwell.

I thought, too, about how much fun it was to be around family members. Many people take such moments for granted because their family is always there. Mine had not been, but just to be with family was refreshing. There had been one awkward moment during our visit when our youngest son Joshua walked up to my dad's brother, my Uncle David. Unwittingly, Joshua called Uncle David "Papa."

David flinched just a bit, and I knew he recognized what I did. It was a slight glimpse of "what might have been" had Dad been alive. Nothing special or unusual, just normal interaction between a grandchild and his grandfather, but it was a relation-ship our boys would never know.

With that thought in mind, I wrote later in the week,

> Times like that create the flood of unending questions that I will never have answered this side of heaven. Did my mother ever think this far into the future? Did she ever think that she would never know her grandchildren?
>
> When my children are much older, we will eventually explain it all to them. It is a part of who we are now. It is irreversible. Maybe this is why I have finally realized the impact of forgiving my mother. Yes, I forgive because Jesus tells me to forgive. But what if my children look me in the eyes someday and ask, "Daddy, did you forgive her?" I want to be a Christ-centered man for my children. I don't want my boys to grow up and see me as a man full of anger and resentment. I want them to see first-hand the healing power of Christ. I want to tell them that the Bible is true. He is our Savior, and you really can "do all things through Christ who gives you strength."

During a teachers' in-service orientation session prior to the beginning of the new school year, I stood once again in front of the faculty and staff. I told them that the date had been set for the long anticipated visit with my mom, and I asked them for their prayers. My colleagues at the school were tremendously supportive, and they not only prayed for Lisa and me that day, but I knew I could count on their prayers as I stepped through the doors of that prison.

As the date for the visit with Mother approached, Lisa and I tried our best to keep life as normal as possible for ourselves and for our boys, but things popped up constantly. During the first week of the 2009 school year, Zachary's second-grade teacher asked his class to write a project, "All About Me," and on the last page they were to answer a question: "If I could wish for anything in the world, what would I wish for?"

In Zachary's hardly legible handwriting, he scrawled, "I wish my grandmother would get out of jail."

CHAPTER 18

The First Visit

For more than ten years, God had been setting me up, conditioning me, and getting me ready to see my mother. The last time I had seen Mother's face was in 1986 at the Memphis courtroom where she had been sentenced to death. Over the years, occasionally our pastor had suggested that I might want to go visit Mom. I rejected those overtures unequivocally, and without a trace of guilt. Then, after Lisa and I were married, every so often I mentioned to her that—perhaps, at some time in my life—I might want to see Mother face-to-face before she died. Lisa always encouraged me to do what God was leading me to do, but she never tried to shame or manipulate me into visiting Mom, nor did she pressure me or push the matter in any way.

Taking a job teaching in prison was a pivotal position God used to nudge me closer to Mother, opening my eyes to a world I had seen only in movies. I quickly discovered that the reality of prison life was a far cry from the Hollywood images in my mind. The inmates I taught there were real people, not caricatures drawn from crime shows on television. Many of inmates were bright and accomplished; the only difference between them and me was that their sins and mistakes had resulted in prison sentences.

Meeting Steve Wilson at Christ Presbyterian Academy and discovering that he had been ministering to Mother in prison for more than a decade was another turning point. How could this man who wasn't even related to Mother love her so much? And how could I as her son refuse to see her?

Most of all, the question that haunted me was: What am I going to tell our own children when they ask me, "Daddy, you tell us that we need to forgive others. Have *you* forgiven Granny Gaile?"

All along the way, God was speaking to me that a visit with Mom was inevitable. Every time I backed away from the thought, God brought it back to me in a different form, or through a new circumstance. When I flinched, or reneged on a commitment—complaining that I was too busy, or throwing away another round of prison visitation applications that Steve Wilson had given me—rather than castigating me, He continued gently leading me, inexorably, irrevocably toward the Tennessee Prison for Women.

Now that I had finally decided to go, I didn't want my visit with Mom to be a secret so prior to the scheduled date, Lisa and I sent out a blog and an e-mail to relatives, coworkers, and to some of our former friends in Memphis, including members of the congregation with whom we formerly worshiped. I briefly informed them that I was planning to visit Mom in prison for the first time and I solicited their prayer support. Many wrote back words of encouragement and promised to pray for me.

As hard as it might be for others to understand, I knew I needed to express forgiveness to her. If the state still executed her for her crime, at least she would go to the grave knowing that I no longer was eaten up with bitterness and resentment. But my thoughts weren't completely altruistic; I needed to express that forgiveness whether she received it or not.

The night before the visit, Lisa was nervous and I could tell she felt protective for me. Over the years, often in the middle of the night, she had been awakened by my agitated tossing and turning in bed when I had been reliving the events surrounding Dad's murder. We sometimes talked into the wee hours of the morning after those bouts of late night inner turmoil. She prayed for me again and again that God would take away the memories that haunted me. She worried how the visit with Mom might affect me. What was I going to be like when we walked out of the prison? "Please, God," Lisa prayed, "don't let Stephen be hurt any more than he already has been."

Now, as we considered what we might encounter the following day at the prison, Lisa asked me, "Are you nervous?"

"No, I'm not," I replied honestly.

"What are you going to say?"

"I don't know," I answered. "All I know is that I am doing what God wants me to do." I had no other agenda. I felt strongly that God would open an opportunity during our meeting with Mom in which I could tell her that I forgave her. I didn't know how long I would stay; I had no pre-planned speech that I wanted to share with Mom. I didn't know if Mom and I would sit there and stare at each other. Lisa and I had no idea how the visit with Mom might go, and I resisted even thinking about it. I simply wanted to keep my heart and mind open to the possibilities.

I had not seen or spoken to my mother face-to-face in nearly a quarter of a century. But for more than a year, I had been telling people that I felt strongly that God was leading me to go visit my mother in prison. Now the appointed day—August 23, 2009—was here, and there was no turning back.

With our first visit to prison looming ahead of us later that afternoon, Lisa and I decided to attend church services as usual the morning of August 23rd. It wasn't simply a sense of duty. We needed the additional spiritual strength we regularly received by worshiping together with fellow believers.

I encountered a completely unexpected experience, however, in the service that Sunday morning, when I became very emotional during the worship time. One song in particular, "Above All," by Michael W. Smith, touched my heart in a powerful way. That was uncharacteristic of me. I rarely respond so overtly in a church service, but I did that morning. I nearly fell apart as the words of the song seared into my heart. Knowing what was in front of us within the next few hours, I was an emotional basketcase. The gravity of the decision we had made pulled heavily on my heart and mind. But I was not about to second-guess it. There was no backing out. We were *going* to that prison.

Immediately after church, Lisa and I met Steve Wilson at the school and rode with him to the prison. We didn't even take time to eat, since we were on a tight schedule, having to fit our visit into the established prison visiting hours, between two o'clock and five. Steve was glad to accompany us, which made Lisa less nervous since he would be with us. Steve had been leading Bible studies in the prison for years; he knew the prison routines, and he knew Mom better than I did at that point.

We approached the gates and quickly discovered that the prison staff was expecting us. We got the feeling that they wanted to facilitate our visit with the least amount of interference. The warden met us at the first checkpoint. The guards nodded politely to us as we walked through the fencing and waited until we were called inside. We signed in, went through a metal detector, were patted down, and stood at the sliding doors that led to the prison.

The first set of sliding doors opened and Lisa and I stepped through and walked forward toward another set of doors. The doors swished closed behind us, adding to the anxiety, before the doors in front of us opened. Although inmates were not permitted to speak to visitors, we noticed several inmates communicating with us by using their eyes, or making subtle gestures indicating that they recognized who we were.

Mom was in solitary confinement, so she was not permitted to come to the usual visiting room, as other inmates might do. We had to go to her in Unit 3, the area housing death row inmates, which entailed walking outside the building, down a passage-way completely enclosed by a chain-linked fence, similar to a tunnel, all the way to the door of her unit.

Lisa and I were ushered to a holding area, facing a long corridor leading to the inmates' cells. Just then, to our surprise, a prison guard accompanied by an older woman dressed in prison garb walked out a door at the end of the hallway. The inmate looked in my direction and even from the distance, we recognized each other immediately. The woman was my mother.

Mother later recalled the moment she first saw me. "The minute I saw him," she said, "even from that far away, I knew. And I pointed at him. I knew him instantly. He looked a lot like Ron."

The guard and inmate moved into a private visiting room. Before I had time to process what I had seen, an older guard spoke to me. "You're Stephen Owens?"

"Yes, I am," I replied, somewhat surprised, since we had already signed in several times getting through the clearances.

"I've heard a lot about you," she said with the slightest trace of a smile.

The guard with Mother directed her to sit at a table until we entered. The senior guard remained in the room.

The moment Lisa and I entered the room was an over-whelming experience for me. There, sitting demurely though nervously at the table was my now gray-haired mother whose face I had not seen in nearly twenty-four years. My eyes locked onto hers and without the slightest bit of hesitation, I opened my arms and moved in her direction. She rose from her chair, and I hugged my mother for the first time in twenty-five years, the last hug we shared being shortly after Dad's funeral.

Mom sobbed openly. "I'm sorry, son," she said as I held her close with her face buried in my shoulder. "I'm so sorry, son." No further explanation was needed. Nobody had to ask, "For what specifically are you sorry?" We all knew. As I later described that moment, it was a raw apology filled with raw emotion, and I accepted it for what it was.

I let go of Mother so Lisa could hug her, as well. Lisa had endured much on the journey to get me here, and as she embraced my mom, tears flowed freely down all of our faces.

We sat down at the table. With little thought of "Where to start? What should we talk about?" the conversation came easily. We talked about Zachary and Joshua; we spoke of other relatives. We talked about all sorts of things. We even talked about Dad, his sense of humor, and some of the funny and enjoyable things we did together as a family. The one thing we did not talk about was Dad's death.

The senior guard seemed to recognize that things were going well, so early on, she leaned over to Mom and asked, "Is there anything you need?"

"No," Mother responded. "I'm fine."

"I'll leave you alone then," the guard said. She moved a large trash can into the doorway to prop the door open and slipped out of the room. We were impressed at the high regard in which everyone in the prison, both staff and inmates, held Mother.

We talked for nearly three hours. I made no guarantees to Mom; I did not promise to help her in any way. I did not tell her that I would ever come back to see her again. But despite the years that had separated us, we connected.

All too soon, time slipped away, and I sensed urgency. The most important reason for my visit had not been fulfilled. I had been convinced that God was leading me to prison to extend forgiveness to my mother, to tell her that I forgave her. I kept waiting for that opportunity to present itself.

Finally, the guard returned and gave us the five-minute-warning, five minutes before Mother would return to death row, five minutes before we would be ushered out of the prison confines, with no guarantee we would ever return. Mother acknowledged the guard, and then turned toward me, with tears quickly welling in her eyes. "I'm sorry, Stephen," she said again. "I know I can't change anything now, but I just need to ask for your forgiveness."

This was it. This was the open door I had been hoping for, praying for, believing that it would nudge open if only slightly. This was what I believed God had sent me to do. I looked my mother in the eyes, and said, "I forgive you, Mom."

Bound up in my expression of forgiveness were the years of hurt and emotional pain my family and I had suffered; all the many ball games I had played without the presence of my dad—or my mother—in the stands; missed birthday parties, and the ache in my heart due to the absence of my parents at so many special events including my graduations from high school and college, Lisa's and my wedding day, the birth of our two beautiful and energetic boys. All of that and more surged through those words, "I forgive you, Mom."

Both Mother and I had received answers to our prayers—hers, that she would see me one more time before she was executed, that she might touch me, talk with me, and ask for forgiveness—and mine, that I might be able to assure her of the forgiveness I had already found in my heart.

Nevertheless, there was awkwardness. Neither of us knew where this visit might lead, if anywhere. Even after expressing my forgiveness to her, I did not promise to return to see her again, and she did not ask me to come. Yet the forgiveness was real; the barriers to our reconciliation had been broken down. Mother and I both knew deep within that something of profound spiritual significance had taken place. And for now, that was enough.

When Lisa and I walked out of the prison, I strode toward the car in silence, entrenched in my thoughts. Lisa hurried to keep up with me. "Stephen! What are you thinking?" she asked.

My words came slowly and with great difficulty. "I don't know that I can really tell you what I am thinking," I said. I felt elated, as though the weight of the world had been lifted off my shoulders, but other than that, I couldn't communicate the overwhelming thoughts and emotions within me. I stopped and looked at Lisa before we got into the car. "All I can tell you," I said, "is that I'll be back."

I felt that God was impressing on me, "You did exactly what you were supposed to do." That alone provided a marvelous sense of release. Beyond that, while there was a bit of closure now that I had finally met with Mother and expressed forgiveness to her, all sorts of new doors had been flung wide open.

Lisa had more questions, the main one being, "What now?"

I didn't know. I had gone into the meeting with no agenda. I knew there would be an opportunity to tell Mom that I forgave her, and that had happened. I had no further agenda following the visit.

Steve Wilson took us back to our car, and Lisa and I sat in silence as we drove home, attempting to process the experience and the emotions of it all.

That night I sent a brief mass e-mail to a number of people who had been praying for us, informing them that the visit had gone well and thanking them for their prayerful concern. I wrote a brief blog and uploaded it that same night.

It was at least a full twenty-four hours before I could even talk about what we had experienced.

"What are you going to do next?" Lisa gently pressed.

"I don't know," I said. "I feel like I have to help. I don't think I have a choice. But I don't know what that means yet."

The visit took place on the Sunday of the first full week of school, so I had to go back to work the next day. Lisa went back to work, as well.

A number of people at the school had known that I was going to see Mom, and many of them had been praying for me. Everyone wanted to know how the visit had gone, but few asked specifically. Several teachers or administrative people came by and asked how I was doing. Nate Morrow, the high school principal, stopped in my classroom early that morning. "Are you okay?"

"Yeah, I'm fine," I replied.

"Well, if you need me to get a substitute in here, just say the word and let me know." I thanked him, and assured him that I was better off working. Nevertheless, I had a difficult time focusing on teaching that day, and I'm sure it wasn't one of my more effective teaching experiences.

That night by the time I got home and we got the kids in bed, Lisa and I were both too emotionally drained to talk through all the issues that the visit with Mom had raised. We talked as long as we could, but before long, we grew silent. "Are we done?" Lisa quipped.

"I think so," I answered, emotionally exhausted.

"Well, I guess we're going to sleep. . . ."

"Yeah, let's try to get some rest."

The first few days following the visit, I walked around in a daze. In some ways, nothing had changed, and yet everything had changed. Prior to visiting with Mom, we knew she was in prison, but she remained merely a distant figure in our minds. She existed only within the realm of the cards and letters we exchanged, filled mostly with information about the kids. Now, I had seen her face; I remembered her eyes. I had heard her voice; I had held her close to my heart. And suddenly the awful impact of the courts' decisions hit me full force.

They are going to kill my mom!

CHAPTER 19

Wrung Out of Hope

The letter came right before Christmas. It was from the Federal Public Defender's office in Middle Tennessee informing us that on December 8, 2009, the Tennessee Attorney General had asked the Tennessee Supreme Court to set a firm date to execute my mom.

Merry Christmas.

Lisa called me at school and gave me the bad news.

Actually, the letter stating that a date for my mother's execution was going to be set was the second stunner I had received from Mother's attorneys, Gretchen Swift and Kelley Henry, of the Federal Public Defenders Office. The first was dated October 5, 2009, when the attorneys wrote to me:

> *Dear Mr. Owens:*
> *I wanted to let you know about a recent development in Ms. Owens's case. In July, we asked the United States Supreme Court to hear Ms. Owens's case, and the Court*

issued an order today saying no. This order essentially marks
the end of any remaining court litigation for Ms. Owens.

At first I thought the words on the legal letterhead had
suddenly gotten blurry, but then I felt the tears welling in my
eyes. The attorneys' letter continued:

> *Around the end of November, we expect the Attorney*
> *General to ask the Tennessee Supreme Court to set an execu-*
> *tion date for Ms. Owens. We expect that the Court would*
> *then set the date for several months out—it could be as early*
> *as April 2010 or as late as June 2010. Around November,*
> *the Attorney General may contact you by phone or letter to*
> *let you know about their request for an execution date. The*
> *prison may also contact you to ask if you are interested in*
> *witnessing Ms. Owens's execution—they are required to do*
> *this by law.*

The thought of watching my mother being executed nearly
nauseated me. I gulped hard, took a deep breath, and continued
reading. I was somewhat surprised at all the ambiguity surrounding the setting of a date of execution; part of that was pro-
cedural, no doubt, but then I realized, this was not an everyday
event for the state of Tennessee either. A woman had not been
executed in our state in more than 189 years. The last execution
of a woman in Tennessee was that of Eve Martin in 1820—by
hanging. While there had been recent executions of males in
Tennessee, even that number was relatively low.

The lawyers' letter then raised an ominous possibility that I
had not previously considered at any length:

> *Around the end of November when the Attorney*
> *General requests an execution date, we expect the media*
> *(which Ms. Owens has tried very hard to stave off over the*
> *years) to begin to be interested in her story and probably in*

you and your brother as well. We will continue to try to keep the media away from you and your brother in particular, as that is and has been Ms. Owens's most important priority, but we also don't have much control at that point.

When I read the letter, my heart sank. The week after visiting with Mother in prison, I had walked around in a dazed state, somewhere between physical, emotional, and spiritual exhaustion and ecstatic euphoria. I had shared the details of the visit with my coworkers at school who asked, and as always asked for their prayers, that the Lord would continue to guide me regarding what my next steps should be—if any.

Now, a mere six weeks later, I was looking at a paper informing me that my mother was likely going to be executed at the hands of the Tennessee Criminal Justice system within the year. I didn't question their right to take such actions, nor did I wish to prolong the agony for everyone involved, but it did hit me hard.

Indeed, if there was any doubt that Mother's attorneys were playing straight with me—that they had not simply sent the letter as a last ditch effort to secure my involvement or my family's in helping with their case—the October letter was confirmed when the second letter arrived in early December.

Mother's attorneys had waited all through the fall to see what the Supreme Court was going to do, whether or not they would consider Mother's case. Lisa and I were aware of these proceedings because Mom had mentioned them to me in a letter. When the Supreme Court refused to hear the case, the last recourse was an appeal to the governor of Tennessee for clemency, asking him to commute Mom's sentence to "life in prison." Now, less than three months after going to see my mom, and feeling good that I had expressed forgiveness to her and we had reached the beginning of reconciliation in our relationship, the letters snuffed the embers of my hope like a bucket of water dousing a campfire.

"Oh, God," I prayed, "How am I supposed to respond to this news? What do you want me to do?"

Disheartened, but too busy with school and coaching to allow myself to wallow in despair, I did not take time to write to Mother following the news. Lisa, however, sent her an uplifting note in which she mentioned my despondency: "Gaile, Please know that we are praying for you and have requested prayers from many others, as well. Stephen is doing okay. He says he is fine but you know, I am his wife and I can look in his eyes and see that he is hurting."

As my wife, Lisa was living through each tumultuous twist and turn of Mother's case along with me, but as a mom, she was also dealing with everyday boys-life issues, so Lisa then did her best to pick up Mom's spirits by including some details of Christmas with Zachary and Joshua:

> *Our Christmas train is surrounded by army men; there is a snowman in the Nativity scene, and baby Jesus is hiding in the candy dish. Gotta love boys. . . .*

> *Lisa: "Boys! Where's Baby Jesus at right now?"*
> *Zachary: "Oh, He's in my backpack."*
> *Lisa: "WHY is Baby Jesus in your backpack?"*
> *Zachary: Because I wanted to show my friend how his butt shows when you turn him over."*
> *Lisa: "GOOD GRIEF, SON!"*
> *Zachary: "Mom, aren't you proud I didn't lie about why I put Him in my backpack?"*

> *Zachary's dinner prayer: "Lord, thank you for this food. Lord, please make Joshua learn to close his eyes when I pray!"*

Joshua's dinnertime prayer: "Lord, thank you for this food. Lord, please help my brother's cough to get better so we can fight."

Joshua: "It's not fair that my name is last on the Christmas card and my stocking is hung up last, too!"
Zachary: "Oh, stop complaining, and just be glad you're in the family!"

No doubt, her grandsons' antics brought a smile to Mother's face when she read them. More and more, she understood that the boys had their dad's sense of humor.

CHAPTER 20

Gaile's Angels

The Bible teaches that angels are messengers from God. Although not in a literal sense, Mom had numerous "angels" in her life, including Steve Wilson, Linda Knott, Pat and Gene Williams, and several other key people that she didn't even know about.

In retrospect, it is easy to see how God surrounded my mother with such angels, people from diverse backgrounds who, for a variety of reasons, took up her cause, caring for her in prison, and fighting within the legal system to help save her life from execution. Although none of the individuals would be so brash as to consider himself or herself as an angel, they were all messengers of God to my mother. It was almost as though God was moving people in the right place into Mother's life at the right time—people, who for the most part, Mother would have no reason to meet, yet she did. Even though I also didn't know it the first time we met, one of those angels was Gretchen Swift.

Gretchen Swift grew up with a passion to help people. She attended Woodmont Baptist Church in Nashville where she and her family were active in the congregation. After high school graduation, she studied at Furman University in South Carolina, where she focused on social work and ways of helping people living in poverty. She was encouraged to go to law school as a route to pursue her passion. While earning her law degree, she recognized that she was different from most of her peers because she wasn't concerned about working for a big-named law firm or making a lot of money. She just wanted to help people.

She was the rare law school graduate, leaving school without a prospect for employment at a law firm. Instead, Gretchen "accidentally" applied for what she thought was a low-level attorney position in the Kentucky Department of Public Advocacy. Gretchen assumed the department was an advocacy group for a social cause. It wasn't. It was Kentucky's version of the Public Defenders' office. God was guiding Gretchen's steps, although it was not in a path she had planned; she interviewed well for the position and was hired. The office was primarily an appeals office for inmates incarcerated in Kentucky prisons, with the attorneys guiding them through their post-conviction hearings.

Ironically, Gretchen was a most unlikely person for such a position. She had little interest in criminal law and her attitude was more prosecutorial in nature, with an emphasis on punishing the perpetrators. In her new position, however, God was showing Gretchen that even convicted criminals are not outside the scope of His love. In the process, God changed Gretchen's heart, tangibly teaching her about mercy and grace through the lives of the inmates she was serving.

Barely a year out of law school, Gretchen applied for and earned a job back in Nashville in the Federal Public Defenders' office, where she became the research attorney for a staff of nineteen. Her duties included assisting all the lawyers in the office. A

supporter of the death penalty, Gretchen did not know initially
that the office handled death row cases until she was called upon
to work on the case of Robert Glen Coe. Mentally ill, Coe had
been given the death penalty for abducting and murdering eight-
year-old Cary Ann Medlin.

Gretchen's team was charged with the responsibility of representing Mr. Coe in his federal appeals and preventing the State
from executing him. Though her heart went out to the Medlin
family, learning about Mr. Coe's sad life changed Gretchen's attitude as she worked to help tell the story to the governor in hopes
of his granting clemency. Getting to know a real person rather
than a mere case study of an inmate evoked a strong sense of
compassion in Gretchen.

Despite her best efforts and those of her colleagues, Coe was
executed in April 2000. The jolt of Coe's execution created some
cynicism within Gretchen, as she realized the legal system is not
always fair, nor is it always the best judge of a person's mind or
heart. Gretchen was becoming increasingly disillusioned with
the death penalty in such cases.

Around 2002, her office expanded, devoting a section exclu-
sively to capital cases, and Gretchen became the research attorney
for that group. Chris Minton, an attorney appointed to handle
my mother's case, went to work in the same office as Gretchen,
the Federal Public Defenders Office, bringing all his cases with
him, including Mother's. Mother's case was not yet at a place
where Gretchen's services were required, so she had not even
seen any of Mother's paperwork, but Chris briefed her on the
basic details.

Gretchen began attending First Baptist Church in downtown
Nashville, closer to her workplace. At First Baptist, Gretchen
met Cecilia Temple, a woman about my mother's age who, like
Gretchen, helped with the church youth program. Cecilia also

visited Mother regularly as a volunteer at the Tennessee Women's Prison. In a casual conversation, Cecilia told Gretchen about a woman she was visiting who was probably represented by the Public Defenders office. "Gosh, I wish you could meet Gaile Owens," Cecilia said. "I think that would be really beneficial to Gaile."

"I would love to meet her sometime," Gretchen said, with nothing more in mind than a friendly visit.

At the time, Mother had already lost appeals at the state levels and was hoping for relief in federal court. It was difficult to maintain a positive, hopeful attitude toward the appeals process after such rejections. Her attorney felt that Mom needed some additional emotional support, so when Gretchen mentioned that she would like to visit Mother, Chris said, "Great! Go for it."

Visitation at the women's prison is quite different than going to a men's prison in Tennessee. For one thing, an appointment is required even for attorneys to visit someone in the women's prison, rather than simply showing up during visiting hours at the men's prisons. The death row inmates were housed in an isolated section of the prison, separated by the long razor-wired, fenced-in tunnel known as "the chute." As Gretchen walked through the general population visiting area then outside through the chute, an armed guard in a truck drove along with her on a gravel track adjoining the tunnel. The mood was intense.

Although Gretchen had visited other inmates in prison as part of her job, she was surprised by Mother. The young lawyer liked her immediately and felt drawn to her. She found numerous elements with which she could relate, including the similarities in her family and ours. Besides our families' mutual faith in Jesus Christ, Gretchen is about the same age as me, and her sister the same age as Brian. Looking into Mom's face, Gretchen's heart overflowed with compassion for the woman about the same age as her own mother.

For her part, Mother did not look at Gretchen as a new lawyer coming to her rescue, a valiant crusader on a white horse riding in at the last minute to help save her life. Quite the contrary, Mother regarded Gretchen as she might a daughter, a new friend, a sweet, sensitive person. They talked about Cecilia and Chris, and their mutual faith, and they soon struck up a close, personal friendship. For several years, Gretchen visited Mother once a month or so. She had no other clients at the women's prison; she went only to visit my mother.

During this time, Gretchen and Mother discussed Brian and me, and Gretchen learned of Mother's desire to see her boys before she died. When Mother told the young attorney about our initial cards and letters, Gretchen was overjoyed. She was young and naïve and had no prior knowledge of the abrasive manner in which my family and I had been treated by other public defenders.

Gretchen's new church was meeting near our home. She had another friend who lived down the street from us. Gretchen felt these things were not coincidences. "God, what are you doing here?" she prayed. "I can't ignore this."

It was out of the kindness of her heart that Gretchen suggested delivering some presents to our son Zachary, and to take some photos that she could return to Mother. Showing up unannounced or uninvited, and delivering birthday or Christmas presents to the grandchildren of death row inmates was not a typical part of Gretchen's job description. In truth, it had nothing to do with her job, but Gretchen was willing to do it out of her love for the Lord and her love for my mother. It was indicative of Gretchen's innocence, that she felt such a gesture would be well received by Lisa and me.

When my response to Gretchen's actions was so negative, Mother's friend was horrified. Gretchen thought for sure that she had ruined any possible restored relationship between Mother and me. When I backed away from writing to Mother after Gretchen's misinterpreted kindness, she sent the letter apologizing for offending us. She felt awful that she may have thwarted the fledgling but growing rapport between Mother and me.

Although Mother's case had now been handled by nine separate lawyers, if anyone ever asked the name of her attorney, she would quickly say, Gretchen Swift. That's because by late 2007, Kelley Henry, Gretchen's supervisor, had assigned Mother's case to Gretchen. Although excited to be able help her friend, Gretchen quickly discovered that she had inherited a mess, from the initial withdrawn plea bargain about which she could do nothing, to the bungled post conviction hearing, which she hoped to address.

In reading the court transcripts, Gretchen got the impression that the prosecutor and his "good old boys" attitude were disgraceful to the practice of law. Moreover, Gretchen was convinced that Mother's lawyers were totally inept. "They were awful." She could not believe that any fair-minded person would accept that Mother's lawyers had done a good job—or even a decent job—for her.

Gretchen honestly thought she could win the appeal for a lesser sentence when she took the case to the Sixth Circuit Court of Appeals in January 2008. The ineffectiveness of Mother's original trial attorneys and her abysmally poor post-conviction representations were beyond question. The prosecutor's withholding evidence of Dad's affairs from the defense, and thus from the jury, was also beyond dispute.

Of course, the facts on appeal were already part of the record, so there was no opportunity for Mother to tell her story, even if she had wanted to do so—which she didn't. Gretchen closed her argument before the Sixth Circuit judges by saying, "The amount of time we have spent discussing this case here today in this courtroom—one hour—is half the time Gaile's attorneys spent investigating her entire capital case before sentencing. Two hours." Two hours to prepare for the sentencing portion of a case in which the jury would render a life or death decision. Whatever the cause—lack of resources, laziness, negligence, or ineptitude—such a dearth of preparation was outrageous.

One of the judges adjudicating the case, Judge Merritt, agreed that the original jury should have been made aware of the evidence of Dad's affairs, especially the letters. He disagreed adamantly that Mother's attorneys had done an adequate job of representing her, and posited that District Attorney Strother was engaging in "plea bargain gamesmanship," hoping to get a high profile death penalty notch, rather than explaining to the jury that Mother had originally pleaded guilty in exchange for a life-sentence. But Judge Merritt's opinion was the dissenting minority in the three-judge panel.

Gretchen and Mother did not win, and the loss was devastating.

To her credit, Gretchen was fighting an almost impossible battle. She had to make the appeal based on the facts of the case that were already on record, nothing more. The attorneys could not bring any new information to the court, until they began preparing for clemency. In the clemency documents, they felt that they had a strong case because they could present additional information, including testimony from experts, even if they did not have the opportunity to bring the truth to the court during the appeals process.

Mother and Gretchen remained close friends despite the legal failures. Mom shared Gretchen's excitement when the attorney got engaged to be married, and Gretchen was glad to bring Mom in on her wedding plans, sharing her joy and excitement.

Meanwhile, Gretchen nursed Mom's case, and by 2008 had become the lead attorney handling the case.

Gretchen had numerous cases, including Mother's, so the intensity of dealing with not only the legal matters but the emotions could be overwhelming at times. Exacerbating her emotions, as Mother's case came closer to the end of her appeal, Gretchen and her husband Rich, who had married in September 2008, discovered about a year later that she was pregnant.

When Gretchen found out that she was going to have a baby, Mother was one of the first people she told. Mother was delighted! Another baby to whom she could be "Granny Gaile."

Gretchen was concerned, however, because she knew she was not going to be able to maintain her level of activity in the case. In the early days of her pregnancy, she frequently became overwhelmed emotionally, thinking, "I won't be able to handle it if something happens to Gaile." When talking with Mother by phone or visiting with her—which she did throughout her pregnancy—Gretchen repeatedly told her, "Just keep hanging on. It is going to be all right."

CHAPTER 21

Another Angel

Katy Varney grew up in Chattanooga where immediately upon graduation she went to work with Jimmy Carter's presidential campaign. She met and worked for Ned McWherter, then Tennessee Speaker of the House, who later became governor of the state. Katy served as the chief lobbyist for the McWherter administration, which was excellent training for a career in public relations. Before long, Katy joined three other friends who had formed a public relations company, McNeely, Pigott & Fox, which over twenty-five years grew to be one of Nashville's premier public relations firms.

A good friend at her church introduced Katy to attorney Brad MacLean, and at least once a year, Brad and Katy got together for a business lunch. On one such occasion, Brad said, "There's an inmate at the women's prison that I would like you to meet. I think you will like her." Katy had worked with Brad on a previous high-profile capital punishment case, and Brad thought that Mother's story might pique Katy's interest.

Katy's opposition to the death penalty was steeped in her life-long religious beliefs, which gave Brad cause to think she would have an interest in meeting Mother. Brad also knew that Katy's husband, Dave Goetz, served in Tennessee's Governor Phil Bredesen's administration as Finance Commissioner. That relationship brought Katy into the governor's presence on a frequent basis, not that she would or could pull a chit with Governor Bredesen, but she had a sense of who the Bredesens were.

Nevertheless, Katy's first meeting with Mother had no agenda other than a meeting between potential friends. Gretchen Swift worked out the details, and Katy trekked out to the Tennessee Women's Prison. In those days, Mother didn't receive many visitors, and really didn't desire a lot of company since the two people she wanted to see the most—Brian and me—weren't interested in visiting her. Nevertheless, Mother was always amenable to accepting visits from anyone introduced to her by Gretchen. Katy had done prison visitation in college, so she was not uncomfortable being behind bars talking with Mother. Katy later said, "Had I been talking with Gaile in any fine restaurant, the conversation would have seemed equally as natural and Gaile would have fit in just as easily." But what struck Katy about Mother was that she could have been comfortable in either place.

At the time of their first encounter, Katy had not read the court transcripts from Mother's case. She simply became a friend to Mother. Mom was warm and receptive and enjoyed Katy's company. Katy was impressed with Mother's intelligence and her graciousness, but astounded that even after all her years in prison, Mother chose to not drag Brian and me through the sludge of her defense. Mother made a statement to Katy that she had told others: "I have made a promise to my sons that I will never speak about what happened. The best thing for me is to go on, and let those chapters of my life remain closed."

In truth, I don't ever remember Mother making that statement to me, but perhaps she did. Or maybe she made that commitment to herself. Regardless, she had stuck to it for more than
twenty years.

Mother was reluctant when Katy wanted to become more
involved in her case and even more reluctant when Katy suggested she tell her story to somebody in the media. They shared
numerous tearful conversations about the subject.

Normally an untiring optimist, as Katy met with Mother
over the months, she occasionally sat up in bed at night, shudder-
ing at the thought that things might not go well, that her friend
may in fact be executed. When she later spoke to Brad about
those feelings, and he was a realist. "You're right, Katy. We may
not be successful here, but we have to try."

Katy wondered what might happen if she could throw the
resources of her company, McNeely, Pigott, & Fox, into the task
of telling Mother's story in such a way as to capture the attention
of the media and the governor. Although she was a key figure
in the company, she knew she could not get more involved in
Mother's case without her partners' knowledge. None of her
partners were aware that Katy had been visiting regularly with
a convicted inmate on death row.

She came back to the office after visiting Mother one day and
gathered her partners together. "I have to tell you something. I've
been doing some volunteer work on my own, and it has evolved
into something that is going to go to a completely different level."
Katy looked around the room into the eyes of her partners, all
of whom were men. "For more than two years now, I've been
visiting a woman in prison, on death row, and they are going to
execute this woman. I feel that I have to step up and take a totally
different role than what I have taken. I can't do it by myself. I
can't write everything that will need to be written or do all that
will need done. I'm going to need a team of people to help me."

Without questions or hesitation, everybody in the room said, "Katy, whatever you need, let's do it." The company engaged its talented pool of people, resources, and influence on Mother's behalf, *pro bono*, free of charge.

The challenge for MP&F was not to reach the world. They did that every day in their business. The real challenge was to build a trust with Mother and to convince her to tell her story to the media, who in turn could take it to the public.

As an expert in public relations, Katy knew many journalists in Nashville, and she felt confident that the right person could tell Mother's story in such a way as to evoke a response from the public that might have an influence on the Supreme Court or, in last resort, upon Governor Phil Bredesen. Convincing Mother of that was another matter entirely.

In another tearful conversation with Mother, Katy looked at her and said, "I can't promise you that a journalist will tell the story the way we hope, but I can promise you this: I will do everything I can to keep you safe, and that telling your story will help to save your life. There are no guarantees that it will work, but I will certainly try. We have only two choices. We can find a good journalist to tell your story and we may not be successful. But if we don't tell your story, we know what the outcome of that will be."

Katy became a regular attendee at meetings of Mother's legal team, which included Gretchen and Kelley, as well as two other unlikely angels, renowned journalist John Seigenthaler, and later, well-known civil rights attorney, George Barrett, with the continued help and insights of Brad MacLean.

Long before I ever visited Mother in prison even once, this group had already met nearly twenty times. The theme of their meetings revolved around communication. How can we tell the story, and how can we get Gaile to help us tell the story? How do

we tell the story to the Supreme Court? How do we tell the story
to the public? What is the best way to approach the governor?

Some public officials were moved more by public pressure
than others. For them a petition filled with thousands of signatures might have an influence. Tennessee's Governor Phil
Bredesen was not one of those. If anything could reach him,
he would be more convinced by the legal aspects of the case—
was the system just, was justice best served? Katy knew that
Governor Bredesen would not be powerfully moved by people
signing a petition, but the team decided to have a petition anyhow, because people wanted to get involved.

Katy's team at MP&F set up a website, Friends of Gaile.com
and before long they had collected more than eleven thousand
signatures on an online petition to the governor asking him to
grant clemency to Mother. The petitioners were not asking the
governor to pardon my mom, but to commute her death sentence
to life in prison.

At the time the case went before the Supreme Court, the
story had not yet been presented to the public. So the group
grappled with whether the presentation should be written in a
more legal fashion, or should they simply tell the story in such
a way that the general public and reporters in particular, would
understand the essential elements of the story and why Mother's
case was truly unique. They recognized that their suggestions
may not bring about the desired result, yet they were convinced
that the only way to bring any public pressure on people who
might be able to help my mother was to tell her story.

It was risky. Mother had lived for years with the idea that
Brian and I and our other family members were better off if the
details of her story remained buried beneath the dust covering
the court records. Katy, however, believed the best way to help
Mother was to blow the dust off all those details, though nobody
knew where the dust might settle.

Quite possibly, in telling the story, even the best journalist might make matters worse. Mother could still be executed, with the resurrected story once again hurting her children and dragging our family—and now, Mother's grandchildren—through more dirt and disrepute.

Everyone involved knew they were playing with fire.

CHAPTER 22

A Friend Indeed

Today, I call him "friend," dear friend, but at the time I first went to visit Mother in prison in 2009, I didn't even know John Seigenthaler. Regarded as one of the most distinguished and respected gentlemen in Nashville, John had worked as editor of the *Tennessean* for thirty years and as a reporter for ten years prior to that. He was also one of the founding editors of the nationally known newspaper, *USA Today*, and has been influential in establishing "The Newseum," in Washington, D.C. Even his political opponents, who might diametrically disagree with some of John's positions, respect John's personal integrity, his truthfulness, and his compassion. Now in his eighties and retired from actively working at the *Tennessean*, John spent most of his time with The First Amendment Center, which he established in 1991 as a forum for discussion of First Amendment rights and values.

Katy Varney's friend, Brad MacLean, knew that John had met with the Governor of Tennessee regarding several other capital cases. Although John's efforts had not been successful in changing the governor's mind, Brad went to John and asked him to look at Mom's case. "John, would you just go out to the prison to meet Gaile?"

That was the last place John wanted to go. As a journalist, he had spent years covering prisons and inmates. Moreover, having grown up in a staunchly Catholic home with seven siblings, John's parents had taught him that killing another human being was wrong, so he had been opposed to the death penalty for most of his life.

John's father had a friend, Gene Woodruff, a roofing contractor who worked for John's dad. When Gene's brother Horace murdered a Nashville police officer and was sentenced to death, Gene approached John's father for help.

One of John's most visceral memories as a child growing up on Nashville's Woodmont Boulevard was looking at his father and Gene having a meeting with John's grandfather in the living room. His daddy was asking Grandfather Seigenthaler, who had some political influence, to plead the case for Horace, that the governor might commute his sentence. It was the first time John had ever seen his father cry. Grandfather Seigenthaler took the case, and eventually, the Tennessee governor commuted Horace's sentence to life in prison. Horace remained in prison for a number of years and operated a radio school, training radio technicians.

Today, in one of the entryways to John's home, the walls are decorated with photographs of John with famous public figures, and there on the wall, is a photo of John with Horace Woodruff, as John interviewed him in prison. Years after Horace's sentence was commuted, he was released on parole, perhaps based in good measure on stories written by John Seigenthaler.

By the time John was a cub reporter, Jim "Droopy" Edwards, appointed by then Governor Frank Clement, was one of the best wardens Tennessee ever had. In those days, guards were still allowed to use whips to enforce prison discipline. John wrote several stories about the cruel form of punishment, and use of the whip was banned in the prisons.

During John's tenure with the *Tennessean*, he spent a lot of time at the state prisons and wrote numerous significant articles about inmates and prison reform.

The *Tennessean* opposed Governor Clement on many issues, and as the editor of the paper, that often put John and the governor at odds. Frank Clement, however, was opposed to capital punishment. He had convinced the State Senate to vote against it, but the State House of Representatives ruled the day and kept it as part of Tennessee law. The governor went to the prison where Warden Edwards had gathered a group of death row inmates.

In what would become one of the most famous statements by any Tennessee governor, Frank Clements said, "I can't save your souls, but I can save your lives. I want you to save your souls." Though the governor reluctantly allowed a few men to walk that "last mile," he never did so without tears in his eyes, or before he had personally gone to the prison to meet with the inmate in an attempt to reconcile his own concerns that the state was making the correct decision, and if the sentence was to be carried out, to help the condemned man be reconciled to God. Clement's courage won great respect from John Seigenthaler.

John learned a lot at the prison, but the one lesson that superseded all others was "Expect to be hustled." Every inmate had a story; most were innocent—in their own minds. They all had received a raw deal, and would not even be in prison if it were not for the actions or attitudes of someone else.

The second great lesson John had learned through his years of covering the prisons was "Expect for your heart to be broken." Heartbreak and working against capital punishment went hand in hand, because rarely did a case turn out well.

Consequently, over the years, John developed a healthy skepticism regarding most inmates with whom he interacted. That's why he really did not want to go to the prison to meet with Mom.

Although Brad knew that he had a philosophical ally in John, especially after briefing him on the details of Mom's case, he could not convince him to meet Mother. Meanwhile, John talked with his wife, Delores, about a matronly woman in prison who had paid to have her husband killed. Delores finally said, "You might as well go meet her, because I can tell it is eating you up, not knowing. Why don't you go? It's going to keep eating at you until you do." So John consented to go along with Brad MacLean and his wife to meet with Mother. There was no agenda to the meeting, in Mother's mind or John's; it was simply an opportunity to get acquainted. Of course, Brad hoped that John might want to become involved somehow in approaching the governor.

Strangely enough, prior to the meeting, Mother was equally skeptical of John. She knew him, of course, as a renowned journalist, and she was also familiar with his weekly television program on Nashville Public Television. What she couldn't figure out was why such a refined and sophisticated person would be interested in her. What was the catch? What did he want?

John and the MacLeans entered the prison, and made their way through the various security clearances. Each step of the way, John expected to be hustled.

When John was introduced to Mother, the first thing she said to him—even before they went into a private room to sit down and talk—was, "You were not on television on Sunday morning."

John was intrigued that Mother had been watching his weekly television program, but her statement tripped his internal "Hustle Meter." He followed Mother and the MacLeans into the room where they sat down at a steel-topped table, Brad's wife to Mother's right, Brad in front of her, and John straight across from Mother, where he could look directly into her eyes.

Brad guided the conversation, and John was relatively quiet, observing Mother carefully as they talked. He was looking for anything that might hint at subterfuge or falseness in Mother, watching carefully for the usual signs of hustle that he had experienced with so many other inmates over the years. He didn't see it or hear anything of the sort. A skeptical, seasoned journalist, John was convinced that Mother was sincere. It was also clear to him that she believed she was going to be executed, and that she was ready to die.

He especially noticed the intensity in Mother when she said, "I am not going to talk to anyone about those things that might cause more pain to Stephen or Brian."

As the conversation progressed, it dawned on John, "This woman can save her own life. If people can understand that she is intelligent and remorseful, all she has to do is to tell her story."

John didn't mean that Mother needed to tell her story in prison, or even to her family members. He realized that if Mother was going to be saved from execution, her story would have to become a public issue.

Near the last part of the meeting, John attempted to press Mother. "People ought to know your story. They need to understand what has happened to you. I'd like to come back and see you, but I need to read a lot more about your case."

Mother welcomed John to come back any time, not really expecting that he ever would.

Shortly after that John met with Katy, Gretchen, and Kelley. Katy had already been going out to the prison, visiting with Mom on an informal basis, simply as a friend.

Both John and Katy had come to similar conclusions about Mother: "She's real. She's human. This is not an act. The one thing she wants is to be reconciled with her children before she dies." But after talking with Gretchen, Kelley, and Katy, John doubted whether Mother would ever have any opportunity of reconciling with Brian and me.

In his second meeting with Mother, John went for the primary purpose of telling her, "You have to allow the press to tell your story. This is a story that needs to be told."

Mother was not at all open to that. In fact, Mother looked back at John, and said, "Over the years there have been many people who have wanted me to tell my story. Oprah Winfrey wanted me to tell the story, but I chose not to do so. If I turned down Oprah, I'm not about to tell the story now. All I've got are my two boys. I've already caused them great pain. I'm not going to do anything else to hurt them. I'm just not prepared to do it."

John left the prison that day discouraged, but undaunted. He and Katy conspired to convince Mother that she did not need to die; that she could, without compromise, tell her story to the media in a controlled manner, and that might cause enough of a public outcry of support that her case could be commuted to a sentence of life in prison. On their best days, reality poked holes in any of the balloons they floated even hinting that Mother would ever be released from prison. But there was at least a possibility, due to the uniqueness of her case that her sentence could be commuted, and rather than the government taking her life, she could live out the remainder of her years in prison.

John met with Mother several times. "You don't have to answer certain questions," he told her. "All we have to do is get a good reporter out here. You are attractive and articulate. If they ask you something that you don't want to talk about, just tell them. And tell them why you don't want to talk about it. 'I love my children and I don't want to say anything about their father.'" Mother still wouldn't hear of it. She did *not* want to talk to any media.

One day John met with Mother without Katy. He felt that he made great progress in convincing Mom to tell her story to a reporter. When he left the prison, he talked with Katy and said, "I think I've got her on the bridge; see if you can walk her over."

Encouraged, Katy agreed, and promised that she'd press Mother to talk with a reporter who could get her story out to the world. Katy did, but Mother backed off the bridge.

Increasingly, John was being drawn to Mother's defense. He consented to consult with Katy, Kelley, and Gretchen whenever they asked—which they did frequently. John didn't want to be become emotionally involved in Mother's case; he had done that for so many years, and now that he was technically retired from the newspaper, he had separated himself from the fracas. Although he possessed a measure of clout as the highly esteemed former editor, he did not want to write the story. Katy contacted Kay West, a highly respected free-lance writer who wrote frequent articles for a local Nashville alternative newspaper, *The Nashville Scene*. Meanwhile, Kelley and Gretchen thought it might be best if someone from the *Tennessean* wrote the story.

To that end, John stopped by the paper's office, and talked with a young female editor who brought along a reporter to talk with him. Ever gracious, John acknowledged that he was not trying to tell them how to do their jobs, but he said, "Let me tell you why I think this is a great story. There is a woman here in Tennessee, Mary Winkler, who not long ago shot her youth pastor husband in the back while he was in bed. She took the gun, and her two children, and left her husband to bleed to death. She was caught, convicted, and spent a few months in a mental hospital, and then she was released. She is now out of the hospital, out of prison, and even now has custody of her children.

"On the other hand, this woman, Gaile Owens, hired someone to kill her husband and he did. She did not wield the gun, but she is going be executed. If I were writing the story, I would contrast those two cases."

John thought the *Tennessean* would see the value and validity of Mother's story. They did but the senior editor was not willing to invest the time and effort in the story if Mother was unwilling to spill her guts and provide details that were previously unknown or at least unpublished. Mother, of course, refused to do that.

Meanwhile John talked with Dwight Lewis, who had covered prisons when John had been the senior editor of the paper. Dwight was now in charge of the editorial opinion pages at the paper.

A few days later, Dwight called John. "They ought to do it, but I don't think they are going to do the story. I just don't think they are going to go there." Then Dwight added, "It won't get done unless you do it."

"What makes you think that?" John asked.

"The editors won't be able to refuse it if you write it," Dwight said.

Angels: messengers from God. John Seigenthaler did what he really never intended to do—his heart got involved in another death row story. And for some reason, he felt compelled to write about it.

John was convinced that, yes, Mother put the wheels in motion to end Dad's life, but as John studied the court records of the trial, the sentencing, and appeals, he became even more convinced that Mother never had a chance, that the legal proceedings in Mother's case had been a disgrace.

Most of all, though, John centered in on the disparate levels of punishment between Mother's case and that of other women convicted of murder or accessary to murder. One of those, Mary

Winkler, had served only sixty-seven days in a mental health facility following her conviction of first degree murder and voluntary manslaughter. Gaile Owens, John noted, was set to be executed.

John decided that it was not necessary to have Mother's cooperation or to quote Mother to tell her story. Indeed, John did not even inform Mother that he was writing a story about her case. When he completed the article, he did something he had never before done in his journalistic career. He called the attorneys and asked them to review the article before publication. "I know there are no errors here," John said, "but there are nuances, and I want this story to be exactly right." Gretchen and Kelley agreed to critique John's article, to fact-check and make certain that everything was absolutely correct.

John's story ran in the *Tennessean* just before Christmas, on December 20. The article evoked a sizable response, most of it favorable to Mother.

With the United States Supreme Court declining to act on Mother's behalf, John and the legal team began meeting more frequently, planning how to best present Mother's case to the governor once a date for Mom's execution was set. There were no other options. Among the subjects that perpetually popped up in meetings was how and where to take Governor Phil Bredesen the information without alienating him and destroying the only remaining chance to save Mother's life.

Like Katy, John knew the governor personally. John had met with Governor Bredesen on at least two cases in which they had sat down privately, in face-to-face, knee-to-knee conversations about death penalty cases. In both instances, the governor had begun the conversations by looking John in the eyes and virtually saying, "Now, John, you know where I am and I know where you are. I'm always glad to talk with you, and I'm going to listen to you, but . . . you know where I am and I know where you are." Although the governor was fair and compassionate, he was not easily moved.

John had also met with the governor's legal counsel along with various groups opposed to the death penalty. He had the utmost respect for Governor Bredesen, but had little hope of moving the governor toward clemency.

John thought that it would be better to have a lawyer present the case to the governor, rather than someone from the media. The governor had given attorney Jim Neal an opportunity to speak to him about commuting another capital case, and although Bredesen had declined to commute the sentence, he had at least considered it.

John had another "angel" in mind, esteemed civil rights attorney George Barrett who had made history as a Southern attorney taking on school desegregation cases, defending students and their families. John and George had been classmates at Father Ryan High School in Nashville. They both had the same view on the death penalty.

George Barrett had recently spoken positively about the governor and in opposition to a class action lawsuit brought by some fellow lawyers against Tennessee Governor Phil Bredesen over his cutbacks on the TennCare healthcare program. John called Barrett and gave him a brief summary of the basics of Mother's case and asked him if he would be willing to join them for a more detailed discussion. Once they had piqued Barrett's interest, John said, "It has to be pro bono, George. She has no money."

Despite the enormous odds, George Barrett agreed to look at the case and help as best he could. "What exactly would you like me to do?" he asked.

John leveled with him. "At some point, we will need you to go to Governor Bredesen on Gaile's behalf," John told him.

"Okay, I'd be willing to do that," George replied.

"We are not going to make some public spectacle," John added. "Nor are we going to mount a letter-writing campaign to the governor, attempting to sway his opinion. We have too much respect for Governor Bredesen to do that."

As John Seigenthaler later said, "The message we wanted to send to the governor of Tennessee was simple: You are an intelligent, fair minded human being. What has happened to this woman has been unfair. The system has been unfair to this woman. For reasons unique to her case, this woman deserves your consideration."

Several other signs gave the legal team a measure of hope. By that time, I had been to visit Mother and John, Katy, and the attorneys were elated. They felt if I, as a victim of Mother's crime, could be persuaded to join them in their efforts to save her life, it could have tremendous impact.

George set up a meeting with the governor. The night before the meeting, John called George, just to brief him and help him focus on the important points.

George was exasperated with the cautious editor. "Seigenthaler, I have got the message!" he fired back at John. "Now do you trust me with this or not?"

"Yes, I do," John replied politely.

"Well, don't try to write a script for me!" George retorted in feigned reproof. "I'm going to go in there and tell the governor what he needs to know. Do you know that I know what he needs to know?"

When George came out of the meeting with the governor, he was reluctant to be too optimistic, but John was encouraged that the governor had given George so much time, even though he did not indicate what he planned to do about Mother's case, if anything at all.

While the public outcry for her commutation increased, joined by churches and a plethora of organizations trying to eliminate domestic violence, Mother sat quietly in prison. Mom had found forgiveness and had established a genuine relationship with God by placing her faith completely in Christ. Although she was not opposed to the legal machinations the public defenders and their fellow angels were attempting on her behalf, she had resigned herself to the fact that she would probably never leave prison alive, that more than likely, she would be executed. Each day she was thrilled to be alive, but she was ready to die. When you think about it, that's a good way to live.

CHAPTER 23

The Return

I didn't go back to see Mom until February of 2010. The gap between visits wasn't because I was unconcerned about her. I really needed to know that I was being led by God, doing what He wanted me to do rather than merely motivated by emotion. I recognized that this process could be costly to me, as well as to Lisa and our kids, so I was cautious, and wanted to step carefully. I took each step tentatively, almost reluctantly. I was walking into the unknown.

The reconciliation in Mother's and my relationship was real, but nonetheless fragile. It was still in its infancy, and we had a lot of room for growth. We both recognized that no matter what, our relationship would never be what it might have been had Dad not been murdered. Beyond that, I had lived a major portion of my life first in a world of illusion perpetuated by my mother, then in a world completely without her, so picking up with her as an adult was almost like meeting a stranger for me. We had to start from scratch.

At no point did I make a rash, abrupt decision that I would now be involved with Mom's legal team meetings, or more involved in fighting for her sentence to be commuted. Yet, increasingly, getting involved in Mother's case seemed inevitable to me. Although I had no idea what that might look like, I genuinely believed that my involvement in Mom's case would somehow glorify God.

Still, I had deep concerns. During that visit with her, I spoke bluntly with Mother. "Do you realize what a step of faith this is for me?" I asked her. "Do you totally understand what I am doing here?" I didn't sugarcoat it. If she didn't understand what was at stake—that I was laying the lives of Lisa and our children on the line, as well as my own, in dealing with the gut-wrenching emotional issues that we had avoided up to this point—I wanted to make sure that she heard it out of my mouth.

"If I get involved in trying to reestablish our relationship, and maybe even trying to get your sentence commuted, and you are not completely truthful with me, I cannot continue our relationship." I knew that if our relationship was to move forward, I expected nothing less than absolute truth and honesty from Mother. I told her, "There's no room to be gray. You have to be completely truthful with me." I didn't expect Mother to reveal anything new about the murder case, or discuss any previously unknown details about Dad, but I emphasized to her that even the slightest compromise with the truth could set back our relationship, and destroy any progress we had made recently.

I wasn't worried whether or not she could be saved from execution. As largely as her death sentence loomed over every decision, I recognized that Mother's life—like all of our lives—was in God's hands. But at the same time, I wanted to be clear with her that I wanted no surprises from her.

I was stepping out on thin ice, and I knew it. I didn't have a twenty-five-year relationship on which to build. My relationship

with Mother was merely a few months old, based on some relatively superficial cards and letters, and a few hours of conversation. My trust was not in Mother or even myself. My trust was
in God, that He was the one leading me to become involved,
and that somehow He would be honored through it all. That is
where I had to live.

Because of that, I discovered that through it all, my faith was
growing deeper and stronger. My first thought was always, "God
is not going to allow this to be something bad." Not that I was
convinced that Mother's sentence could ever be commuted or
that she would not be executed. But I believed He would use this
situation for good, that He would turn things around and make
it okay. My attitude was: It may not turn out the way I want, but
it is going to be okay.

Near the end of our visit, Mother mentioned that Gretchen,
her lead attorney was soon to have a baby, but she was still visiting Mom on a regular basis, even though her superior, Kelley
Henry, was now handling her case. Encouraged by the fact that
Mother and I had seen each other face-to-face, Gretchen wondered if I might be willing to write a letter to the governor letting him know that, and expressing some level of support. Mom
wasn't exactly sure what Gretchen thought might be helpful.

"Give me her phone number and I will call her," I said.

"Really?" Mother could barely hide her surprise.

"Yes, I'll call her."

Apart from that, Mother did not ask or encourage me to
get involved in her case. In fact, at first she resisted the idea.
She knew that if I poured myself into trying to get her sentence
commuted, and our efforts failed, then she would indeed be
executed, but my family and I would be left to deal with the
ramifications of that.

It was a risk for all of us, but one that—a step at a time—
Lisa and I were willing to take.

CHAPTER 24

The Letter

The journey from being entrenched in bitterness and resentment, not caring about Mom at all—including whether she lived or died—to fighting for her life was an arduous trip, but one that quickly turned into a beeline. One of my initial steps was rather innocuous, simply writing a letter of support.

When Mom's attorneys received word in December 2009 that the Attorney General had asked the Tennessee Supreme Court to set an execution date, they immediately put together a motion requesting an extension of time—until February 5, 2010—to respond. As they were permitted to do in their response, the attorneys set forth five reasons why Mother should not be executed but that her sentence instead should be commuted:

1. evidence establishing that Ms. Owens was a possible victim of abuse;
2. evidence demonstrating that Ms. Owens's trial lawyers utterly failed in their representation of Ms. Owens;

3. evidence showing that Ms. Owens's post-conviction attorneys . . . squandered the hard-fought opportunity to present expert testimony on behalf of Ms. Owens by hiring
   an incompetent witness to testify in post-conviction;

4. evidence establishing that the same prosecutor who the
   Supreme Court just criticized for withholding evidence
   from Vietnam Veteran Gary Cone, also misled the trial
   court and trial lawyers about the existence of salacious
   love letters between the victim and his lover, thereby
   preventing Ms. Owens from proving her husband's infi-
   delity at trial;

5. evidence that the imposition of the death penalty in this
   case is truly disproportionate.

While some might regard such a motion as an exercise in
futility, it was truly a godsend. The extension was granted, and
the state Supreme Court took time to consider the issues raised
by Mom's attorneys.

In the meantime, God was softening my heart toward my
mom, and the recent news about the soon-to-be-set execution
date gnawed at me, as well.

I had never met Mom's attorneys, but after our visit in
February, Mother gave me Gretchen's cell phone number and
told Gretchen that I was going to call her, that I might be willing
to write a letter to the governor in support of their efforts.

I dialed Gretchen's number. Gretchen later told me that when
she saw my name on her caller I.D., she said to her husband,
Rich, "Oh, my gosh, he's calling! He's calling me!" She pulled
herself together and answered the phone quite professionally.

I asked her several basic questions about what sort of letter I
could write that might be helpful to Mother. We talked for more
than an hour, and Gretchen told me to simply write from my
heart, addressed to Tennessee's Governor Phil Bredesen.

On Valentine's Day, 2010, a few days before the twenty-fifth "anniversary" of Dad's death, I wrote to Mother informing her that I had made contact with Gretchen:

> *The days since we visited with you have been busy. I have had basketball games and I talked to Gretchen last Monday. I have actually talked to her a couple of times now. We have completed the letter. I am going to send them to the governor and to your attorneys tomorrow. I am actually going to meet Gretchen and hand deliver the copy to her tomorrow. Gretchen said she thought that it could only help, but she did not know how much. I am including a copy for you in this letter. Honestly, I know that I am doing the right thing; however, there are moments of nerves and anxiety. I haven't told Brian and Aunt Carolyn because I feel, as Lisa told me the other day, this is my journey. Just like I did before I visited you the first time, I have to lay all of that at God's feet and let Him handle it.*

Gretchen had emphasized that time was of the essence as they were preparing a package of materials that would be taken to the governor presenting the case why he would have solid reasons to commute Mother's sentence to life in prison. She wanted to include my letter in that presentation. "If you can write it soon, I'll meet you anywhere in town," Gretchen offered, "to get the letter."

"Well, I don't want to meet at school," I said. I suggested meeting her in a grocery store parking lot. Since Gretchen and I had never previously met, we told each other what cars to look for, and basically how we might recognize each other. She called several friends and asked them to pray for her during our meeting.

I met Gretchen after basketball practice on a school day, wearing a gray sweat suit and sunglasses; I looked for her car and the type of person she had described. I spotted her, waved, and pulled my car into a spot near hers. I got out of the car and adjusted my sunglasses. I was tired and already deeply emotional, the glasses hiding my tears. The attorney seemed emotional as well. She struggled to maintain her composure as we shook hands, formally and quite professionally.

"I can't imagine what this has been like for you," Gretchen said. Her kindness in her voice surprised me, but then she surprised me even further when she said, "I've been praying for you."

Gretchen later said that she wanted to hug me, that it was so weird meeting for the first time, meeting someone for whom she had prayed for more than eight years. Of course, I didn't know that, and Gretchen was trying desperately to maintain proper decorum and not to say or do anything that would be professionally inappropriate. So we maintained a rather terse cordiality at first. She seemed almost as nervous as I was.

I handed her the brief letter I had written to the governor, expressing my desire that he have mercy on my mother. I felt like a drug dealer passing off contraband during a clandestine meeting in a parking lot. "I hope this letter is good enough and what you want. I wasn't quite sure what you wanted me to say. Is this what you meant?" I asked. I really wasn't sure how to go about writing such a letter, but had tried to follow Gretchen's instructions she had given to me by phone.

Gretchen opened the letter, let her eyes scan down through it, and smiled. "Yes, this is perfect," she said. "This will really help, Stephen. Thank you." I got the feeling that as long as my signature was on the letter, it wouldn't have mattered much about my grammar or content. Of course, it did, but Gretchen was obviously happy to get anything at all from me.

We talked briefly about Mom, and Gretchen seemed different from other lawyers with whom I dealt regarding Mom's case. She seemed genuinely concerned about Mom not only as a client, but as a person; I could tell that she was emotionally invested in Mother on a personal level. She thanked me again, and I thanked her, and we parted ways.

Although I had no idea at the time, Gretchen later told me that she drove out of the parking lot, with her heart pounding, and nearly shouting to herself, "Oh, my gosh, I can't believe that just happened!" She had been praying for years that I might be reconciled with my mother; more recently she had hoped and prayed that I might get involved in Mother's case somehow. Now, I had. *Everything has changed,* Gretchen thought.

CHAPTER 25

Living Out Loud

Lisa and I had numerous discussions about whether or not I should get more involved in Mom's case and she was incredibly supportive. "Stephen, I cannot give you an answer about what you should or should not do," Lisa said. "But whatever you decide to do, I'm with you."

Then she hit me between the eyes with a zinger. "If God is leading you to do something, how can you say no to that?" Often we would discuss how we teach other people about God's love yet how could I sit back idly and just watch what was happening with Mother without even making an attempt to save her life?

We talked, too, about our boys. I knew the day was coming when I would have to inform our kids about their grandmother. Lisa and I had engaged in conversations about what to tell Zachary and Joshua, and how to tell them. How much did they need to know? We even sought out a counselor who could advise us regarding how to best pass along information about Mother to our kids.

During those days, Lisa and I prayed repeatedly for strength. "Whatever I'm supposed to do, God, please open the door," I prayed, "and I will go through it." I never lost faith, but I prayed many desperate prayers, such as "God, you can't leave me here. I have to know that you are with me. Please show up in my day, and let me know that you are still walking with me in all this." Or, "Lord, however this turns out, you are going to need to be there for us."

Throughout this time, the Lord reminded me in various ways that He was still leading me. He gave me a quiet confidence that we were walking in His will, according to His plan. His word was: "Yes, I'm here. You are still going in the right direction. I'll let you know later what it is all about."

I had not written a new entry to my blog since September 24, 2009, so just before sending the letter to the governor, I had felt compelled to let people know about the new step I was taking, and to ask for their prayers. I briefly informed my readers about the letters we had received stating that an execution date would be forthcoming. Then it was time to bare my soul:

> When we received the letter back in September, it was time for me to make some decisions. Big decisions. Do I continue to walk the journey out loud or do I retreat and seek refuge in my privacy? It is much easier to keep all of this very private and I still feel a certain degree of privacy is vital. But I kept wondering if I was hindering God's plan all in the name of privacy. Was I being disobedient? I felt challenged. It felt like a test of faith. I felt the powerful healing hand of God by forgiving my mother. Now, my mother is facing the real possibility of being executed. Did God really expect me to continue to live out loud and share this with others? Is that really a fair expectation after everything that has happened in my life? But then that

other question comes to mind. What if? What if my life
story leads just one person to accept Christ?

And then there is this question: How do I profess my
faith in God and speak of His amazing grace and love and
do nothing for my mother?

Because she committed a horrific crime that resulted
in the death of my father? Yes, that seems like a solid
justification not to help her. No one would ever blame
me for refusing to advocate for her. In my mind, it is one
thing to offer forgiveness, but it is completely different to
actively fight for her.

So why was I feeling so conflicted? I am not one to
act on emotions with an unclear mind. I have struggled.
I have prayed. The consequences of my actions could be
life-changing. Not everyone will understand my decision.
Maybe no one will understand. Others might be angry with
me. I could risk losing relationships with family and friends.
The struggles continue. I have prayed so hard about this
decision.

This is life or death.

I have chosen to fight for life and I will leave the
consequences to God. I feel in my heart that if I do nothing
at all, then I am making the statement that I want my
mother to die. Lack of action is really an action in itself. It
is an action to watch her die. In my life right now, in this
situation, lack of action is a lack of faith and trust in God.

I do not want my mother to die. My visit with her in
August changed my life.

I will write more about the details later, but again
I am asking you to continue to pray. Pray for my
mother, Gaile Owens. Pray for my family. Pray for those
responsible for making the decisions.

Pray for truth.
Pray for justice.
Pray for healing.

Unquestionably, getting involved in Mom's case was a challenge to my faith. I genuinely needed to constantly examine my motives, and my spiritual understanding. Was I really hearing from God? Or, were these decisions based in my own emotions, or in my own wisdom, or worse yet, from a spiritual perspective, was I walking in the flesh, rather than in the Spirit? Was I operating out of my own selfishness, manipulating people or events to get what I wanted rather than doing what God wanted? I was living in an intense season of personal introspection, and it was a perpetual struggle.

I shared my new feelings with my blog readers on February 20, 2010.

> I desperately want to fight for my mother's life. Our relationship is alive and I can only plea to others not to take this away from me now.
>
> I am uncertain of the path that God is leading me on, but I can tell you that He is showing up every day, and I can see and feel His presence in the people and events unfolding around me. I know the only way I ever would have believed that my mother had changed and reformed her life was to see the evidence face to face. God has revealed this proof and continues to reveal His work to me every time I see her. It is so difficult for me to describe in words. It is real. It is powerful. It is amazing. It is love. It is peace. It is undeniable.

Mother received my letter informing her that I was writing to the governor on February 17. She wrote back a few days later, apologizing for taking so long to respond, but that she had been overwhelmed with emotions. She said she had started several letters to me and had broken down in tears each time.

> *Stephen,*
> *First I want to thank you for your letter to the governor. I would have never asked you to write one. In fact, I have not asked anyone to write one. There have been a lot of people who knew I filed the clemency, but their decision to write was their own making. Just as those who responded to the articles by John Seigenthaler, those that have responded did so of their own accord. I have just laid this last part at the foot of the cross, in God's hands, not mine. Your letter is overwhelming to me. It's not the act of courage to write the letter alone, but your testimony of forgiveness and reconciliation. I have known since our first visit that this could and did only happen because of God.*

Mother's letter caused me to think that it might be helpful for both of us if I allowed her to know a bit more of my thoughts, and especially how God was working in my life regarding our relationship, why I decided to write the letter to the governor, and my involvement in her case. On February 24, 2010, I wrote to her:

> *In regard to the letter [to the governor] I wrote, it is of God's making. I won't rehash all the steps I took in getting to this place, but I will share a little bit with you. When I left after the August visit, I knew that I had changed in several different ways. The following days after the visit, the idea of writing the letter was on my mind. I struggled for months, not because I did not believe that is what God was leading me to do, but because I had to stop worrying about everyone else's opinion. So when we visited last time, I approached it just like the August visit and told God to lead me during the*

meeting. I felt that if this was what God had put on my heart to do, he would make it happen. Of course, that happened in our meeting. I tell you this to show you that, in this whole situation, I will always lay it at God's feet and let him show me the plans he has for me. The last few months, Jeremiah 29:11 has really been on my heart. "For I know the plans I have for you," declares the LORD, "plans to prosper you and not to harm you, plans to give you hope and a future." This verse has been the foundation for the last few years, but especially the last few months. I do not know why I shared this with you, but I felt that you needed to know my journey. I will finish for now, but know that I love you, and no matter what happens down the road, that will never change.

When I told Mother during a telephone conversation that I wanted to get involved in her case, I was expecting her to be elated, but I was totally wrong. Mom was terrified. "Stephen, please don't do that," she said quietly. "I don't want you to do that." Although she didn't want to voice it, her primary concern was: If Stephen gets involved and becomes really invested in this case, who is going to catch him if things don't work out well? He hasn't been in my life for all these years, and now he's here at the end, and what is that going to do to him if my sentence is carried out?"

We talked further and Mom relented when she realized that I had made up my mind. "Well, you do what God wants you to do," she said.

I later learned that Mom was intensely concerned for me, especially how I might be affected if her death sentence were carried out. She was okay about herself; she was prepared emotionally and spiritually. She knew the moment she was executed, she'd be on her way to heaven. She was at peace and resigned to what might happen to her, but she was worried about me. She had not wanted me to get involved in her case, and now that I had, she fretted what might happen to me if she were executed after all.

Too late, Mom. I'm in.

I called Mom's attorneys' office. "I'm willing to help if you think I might be of any value. Is there anything that I can do?" I asked Gretchen. I honestly didn't know whether I could be of help or not, but I recognized my unique position as both a victim of the crime and a supporter and son of the perpetrator.

Gretchen was excited but controlled her emotions as much as possible. "When can we meet?" she responded quite professionally.

Gretchen, Kelley, Lisa, and I met at a restaurant to talk. I had delivered the letter to Gretchen earlier but I had never met Kelley. They both seemed nervously excited, nervous about not wanting to offend me in any way, but excited that Lisa and I were on board and willing to help them. They gave us a brief run-down on what they expected to happen next—and how they planned to proceed with a more public approach, hoping to provide the necessary legal information, as well as setting a public stage in which Governor Bredesen might be willing to commute Mother's sentence to life in prison. The women emphasized that one of their volunteer members of the "legal team," Katy Varney, was married to the governor's finance commissioner, and Katy had indicated that the governor was not likely to be greatly influenced by public opinion. Gretchen and Kelley felt it was worth it to mount a grass roots effort, anyhow.

"I'm in," I told the attorneys that night. "I will do whatever I need to do, but I will never go in front of the cameras." I still carried the stigma of my repulsive encounter with the press back at Mother's trial. The attorneys simply nodded and smiled.

I left our meeting that night impressed with the deep level of commitment of the two young lawyers, but also deeply concerned that their efforts, and now mine, too, might all be in vain.

CHAPTER 26

Death Knell

Over the next few weeks, I talked with the attorneys at every opportunity, sometimes several times each day, five or six days each week. While we were basically on hold throughout the spring of 2010 waiting for the inexorable Supreme Court announcement, I talked with Gretchen and Kelley frequently about their plans for what steps could be taken next.

On April 19, 2010, our next move was determined by the Supreme Court of Tennessee. The court rejected Mother's attorneys' request that her sentence be modified. While denying any modification or commutation of the sentence, the court also set the time and date for Mother's execution.

Kelley sent a text message to me on my cell phone at 2:17 p.m. indicating that she needed to talk with me immediately. I knew that wasn't good. I had a room full of high school students in my classroom, so I stepped outside the classroom and into my office to take the call. "Stephen, I have some bad news,"

Kelley said. "The time and date for your mom's execution has been set for ten o'clock at night on September 28, 2010."

The news hit me like getting punched in the stomach by a prizefighter. I instantly felt sick to my stomach and my emotions welled within me. When I ended the call, I fell apart. I just bawled. I left the classroom area and went into one of the administrative offices, and asked the principal, Nate Morrow, to cover my class until I could pull myself back together. After a while, I regained my composure and went back into the classroom to finish out the day.

I tried to carry on doing the things I had always done, which was always my stance, especially in front of our kids. But this was uncharted territory. Having a firm execution date changed everything. Prior to this, we all knew, and even anticipated that someday, my mother was going to be put to death. Now, we had an actual date on the calendar when the deed was set to occur. The government really planned to kill my mother at 10:00 p.m. on September 28, 2010.

Gretchen Swift was especially devastated when the Supreme Court set the date of Mother's execution to September 28, the same day as Gretchen's and her husband, Rich's wedding anniversary. Her father, a godly Christian man, called to encourage her. "Don't worry, Gretchen," he said. "I don't think for a moment that God will allow Gaile to be executed on a day that is so special to you and so significant to your life." Gretchen appreciated her Dad's comforting and uplifting message, and as soon as she got off the phone, she wiped the tears from her eyes and drove out to the prison to console Mom.

Kelley had suggested that we get together as soon as possible to discuss our next move. She notified Gretchen, who was still out on maternity leave, as well as Katy Varney, George Barrett, and John Seigenthaler. Katy Varney suggested we meet that night because the legal team felt it was imperative to have a press conference at George Barrett's office the next day, and they wanted me to put together a statement that I could present to the media.

Lisa and I met with Katy and Kelley as soon as I could get there after school. We talked about my reservations in dealing with the media. They were going to have the press conference anyhow, but they felt it would be stronger if I were to speak out on Mother's behalf.

As I previously mentioned, I had a lot of anxiety talking to the press and had already told the others that I would do as much as I could but did not want to speak in front of the cameras. After all that had happened during Mother's trial, I had a great dislike for the media, but I was also concerned for my Aunt Carolyn and brother. I knew that once I stepped in front of the cameras, the spotlight would also shine on them and I did not want to cause pain and anguish for them. Lisa kept suggesting that I pray and seek God's wisdom and guidance on what would be best to do. Ultimately, despite my discomfort in dealing with the media, I felt that God was moving me to step out in that direction. This was something I must do.

Meanwhile, as Katy worked with me to help prepare my statement appealing to the governor, John Seigenthaler and George Barrett were already discussing my role in the planned press conference. George said, "We'll be better off to let Stephen make a statement, let him thank the governor for his consideration, and then get him out. Kelley, Gretchen, and I will handle the questions from the media."

That was fine with me.

CHAPTER 27

Full Court Press

The night that the execution date was set, an article ran in the Memphis newspaper saying that a press conference was scheduled for the following day. The article said that I had called a press conference, which, of course, I had not. The family in Memphis knew that I had been visiting Mom in prison. I had told them so during one of Lisa's and my visits with our extended family. But it was the elephant in the room; nobody wanted to talk about it. And nobody there was supportive. They didn't mind me visiting Mother, but getting involved in trying to save her life? That was unimaginable. I had no reason to believe they would be happy about the public statement I was about to make.

Since it was a work day for me, Lisa met me at the school, where Nate Morrow and Drew Maddux, my friend and supervisor, offered to go with us. We took Nate's car so I could focus on what I wanted to say.

The mood in the car was pensive, as everyone knew that I was nervous about going in front of the media. My last encounter with the press had been in 1986, with cameras flashing in my face as I walked in and out of the courtroom in Memphis, testifying against my own mother. Even now, I didn't want to do a press conference. I felt compelled to do this; if I was serious about trying to help my mother, I had no choice but to appeal to Governor Bredesen, because the execution date had been set. Riding in the car with Lisa, Nate, and Drew on the way to the press conference, I was nervously immersed in my thoughts, contemplating my appeal to the governor to spare Mom's life.

The members of the legal team agreed to meet in a back room at George's office before the members of the media were allowed to stake out their territory. Several people had already arrived when Lisa and I entered the building.

Lisa noticed an elderly, white-haired gentleman walking down the hall. "That's John Seigenthaler," she whispered.

I nodded.

When John came into the room, I immediately stood to meet him and to shake his hand, but John did not wait for me to approach him. Instead, he came across the room, and with tears welling in his eyes, he opened his arms and hugged me like a father might hug a long-lost son.

Still embracing me, John said, "It is so good of you to be here, Stephen. I'm so glad that you are involved. I know you are going to play a large role in this, and we are privileged that you are willing to help." I didn't know much about John Seigenthaler, but rather than meeting the sagacious, Yoda-type fellow I assumed he would be, I felt as though I had just met the most gracious man in the world.

At the press conference, I also met Pat and Gene Williams for the first time. The couple had been visiting regularly with my mom in prison for more than thirteen years. Laid back and soft spoken, they were nonetheless strong in their faith, loving, and kind. I never questioned their love and concern for Mother. Pat and Gene's work at the prison was on a voluntary basis.

Also in attendance was respected Nashville singer/song-writer, Marshall Chapman, who had met Mother when the singer had done a concert at the Women's Prison, and had kept up a correspondence with Mother ever since, along with the Public Defender, Kelley Henry, and public relations expert, Katy Varney.

And then there was George Barrett. Like John, George was an octogenarian who still put in ten-hour work days five to six days a week, even though he was technically "retired."

"I didn't go to law school to be a corporate lawyer," he was fond of telling anyone who would listen. "I went to law school to represent working people." For more than five decades, he had done that and more, waging court battles on behalf of civil rights groups, labor unions, teachers, convicts, hospital patients, protestors, and others who might seek his help because they were considered underdogs or second-class citizens. Adamantly opposed to capital punishment, George had worked on several high-profile death penalty cases in Tennessee.

A wide-shouldered man, balding with gray hair on the sides of his head, George still cut a swath of sartorial splendor, always dressed immaculately. He greeted Lisa and me warmly, but very businesslike. There was work to be done. He gathered everyone together and gave us a quick run down on how the press confer-ence should go: He would open the event, and introduce the key players, and then have me read a statement. "Stephen, as soon as you are done speaking," George said, "I want you to go out the back door. Don't stop. Don't allow anyone to distract you. Get out of the office and wait in the back room. We'll handle the questions from there."

When the time came for me to speak, I was nervous because I knew this was our one chance to reach the governor and the public at the same time, but I felt oddly at ease. I knew I was doing what God wanted me to do, and the results were in His hands, not mine, or even the governor's.

Nevertheless, I could feel the tension in my voice as I sat at the table and addressed my remarks directly to Governor Bredesen. Reading from my notes, I entreated:

> "My statement is a public plea to Governor Bredesen to spare my mother's life. Please do not leave me with the responsibility of looking into my sons' eyes and explaining that their grandmother was executed. Please do not allow a death penalty to be the legacy of my family. I am asking for your mercy. I am the face of the victim in this tragedy.
>
> "Gaile Owens is my mother. I am her son. Please do not take this from me. There is no justice in taking her life. There is no justice in denying the healing power of forgiveness. Last year I walked into the Tennessee Prison for Women and saw my mother for the first time in more than twenty years. I looked my mother in the eyes and told her I forgive her."

As soon as I completed my statement, the lawyers whisked me away from the desk, and out the door. I never heard a single question asked by members of the media.

The other key people in the room remained to answer questions and to be interviewed by the press, and they handled the queries with tremendous poise.

Following the press conference, we received an outpouring of support from people wondering how they could help. I soon found myself meeting with the legal team almost on a weekly basis, as we discussed the best ways to capitalize on the publicity we had received and generate even more.

The legal team was a spiritual cornucopia. John Siegenthaler had strong Roman Catholic roots; Kelley was a Methodist; Katy, a self-proclaimed "bleeding heart liberal," was Episcopalian, and Gretchen, a Southern Baptist. Thankfully, they understood when I constantly emphasized, "God has brought me to the table; otherwise I would not be here." Moreover, even when conferring with them, I maintained a simple standard for deciding what I would and would not do. I never made an on the spot decision. In every situation, I prayed at least overnight, asking God for direction. If I felt God wanted me to do it, I would. If I did not feel it was something God wanted me to do, regardless of the persuasive personalities in that room, I refused.

No doubt, the members of the legal team—all unpaid volunteers except for Public Defenders Gretchen and Kelley— must have grown tired of my hyper-spiritual tone, but they never seemed put off by my faith. Even if they were annoyed at times, they understood that the only way I could move forward with confidence was by following God's leading, rather than my own.

Beyond that, the legal team recognized that no matter what it meant to her own future, even if it meant going to the death chamber, Mom was not going to do anything if she thought it might hurt me. I was especially wary in my initial meetings with the legal team, but any doubts or concerns I may have had about their motivations quickly dissipated. John in particular became a confidant to me, a trusted advisor, a father-figure, and a dear friend. Indeed, other than my mother and Lisa, one of the most significant people God has blessed me to know has been John Seigenthaler.

Ironically, it was not until I became involved with the legal team that I truly came to fully understand what a horrific deal my mother had received from the prosecutors who had tried her original case, and the ramifications of District Attorney Strother's offering Mother a plea bargain if she would plead guilty—which she did—but making it contingent upon Porterfield's pleading guilty, as well, which he did not. I never realized the full ramifications of the plea agreement to which she had agreed, and then had been pulled from her because the murderer, Sidney Porterfield, would not agree to it.

Worse yet, I never truly understood that Mother had pleaded guilty and signed a guilty plea until I read the court transcripts and saw it in her own handwriting. For most of my life, I was given the impression that Mother had never taken responsibility; I had been told that Mother had made excuses and tried to rationalize her actions by blaming Dad. The implication was that Mother had denied responsibility for Dad's death, so any time she came up for various appeals, it always rubbed me the wrong way. Nobody had ever told me—not the prosecutor, family, or friends, *nobody* ever told me that Mother had accepted responsibility for her crime from the get go.

One of the priorities in our discussions at the legal team meetings was always how we could best get Mother's story out to the public, and hopefully engender some good will on which the governor could depend if he were to commute her sentence. John Seigenthaler had already written two articles, one in December 2009, and another in January 2010, that had run in the *Tennessean* and had received positive responses. John was encouraging other writers at the paper to pick up the cause, but the editors were reluctant.

Katy Varney had been in discussions with writers from *The Nashville Scene*, a free, alternative Nashville newspaper. Although the *Scene* didn't have the clout of the *Tennessean*, the editors were always on the lookout for edgy, controversial stories, and more than any other newspaper in town, they would likely give significant space to a story about Mother. The team also discussed sending local television stations stories about Mother, as well.

Originally, the attorneys thought that an article would be written by Kay West, a popular free-lance writer who worked frequently for *The Nashville Scene*. Instead, the initial article was done by Brantley Hargrave, and had a more investigative reporter tone to it, much of which leaned toward the salacious.

When the first of two Hargrave articles came out, Mom's attorneys didn't want me to read it. I knew the article must be troubling when Lisa called and warned me not to read it until I got home from school. The school principal, Nate Morrow, saw me and also cautioned me against reading the article until after school. That simply lit me up even more.

I found the article, read it, and I was furious. I felt that the reporter did a cut and paste job, merely drawing statements from court documents. He also included a generous supply of salacious material regarding the alleged abuse Mom experienced, Dad's alleged affairs, and other less than complimentary details about our family.

Kelley was not nearly as concerned as I was. She called me and said, "We didn't think the article was that bad." The attorneys felt the article was helpful in making the public aware of the conditions that had tipped the scales and caused Mom to take such drastic steps to escape her situation. Kelley was concerned, however, that the sordid detail of the article might cause me to back away from my involvement.

That wasn't going to happen. Although the article upset me, I was committed and nothing was going to change that.

Throughout Mother's long stint in prison, she had never granted an interview to any reporter, locally or nationally. She had turned down requests from national television shows, including an interview opportunity with Oprah Winfrey. John and Katy had been trying to get Mom to do an interview with journalist, Kay West. But when Mother found out that I was not happy about the previous articles, she backed away from giving any further interviews with any reporters.

Because of my own negative experience with the media, and the residual bad taste in my mouth from the recently published articles, I probably would have discouraged Mother from talking to anyone in the media. But with the date for her execution set, and the only remaining hope we had was for the governor to commute the sentence, I saw Katy and John's wisdom in having Mother interviewed by a reporter that we could hopefully assume would write a positive article. I went to visit Mother in prison and told her, "You've got to do this. You don't have a choice. Mother, you have to do this." She was still reluctant, but finally agreed to a "controlled" interview. No doubt, she wouldn't have done even that had I not encouraged her.

Mom acquiesced and allowed Kay West to submit interview questions through Katy Varney and Mom's attorneys. She then answered the questions on paper and sent them back through her attorneys and Kay West wrote a poignant and compelling article, describing Mother's incarceration and the injustice of her upcoming execution date. The article struck a chord in the public's heartstrings, creating an even greater groundswell calling for the commutation of Mother's sentence.

During the spring of 2010, Lisa and I tried our best to stick with our family routines and maintain some sense of normalcy with the boys. We kept them involved with school and church activities, as well as elementary school sports.

Preparing the appeal to the governor required enormous amounts of time on the part of Gretchen, Kelley, Katy, and the rest of our team. Often, after teaching school all day, and coaching basketball in the evening, I'd race downtown to meet with them, meetings that sometimes ran late into the night.

We didn't try to explain everything to the boys, but they knew I was in a lot of meetings. Sometimes they asked questions Lisa wasn't expecting. One such night, I was meeting with our legal team working on the clemency run, and Lisa was home alone with the boys, getting them ready for bed.

Zachary started crying.

"What's the matter?" Lisa asked, wrapping him in her arms.

"I'm thinking about G.G." Zachary said through his tears. "I'm afraid that G.G. isn't going to go to heaven."

"Why would you say that, Zachary?"

"I'm not sure G.G. believes in God," he said.

Lisa hugged Zachary closely. "Yes, G.G. does know God, Zachary; she has accepted Jesus as her Savior."

In the midst of Lisa's conversation with Zachary, Joshua came in and saw that his brother was upset. "What's wrong with Zachary?" Joshua asked.

Lisa tried to explain simply.

"Oh, G.G. is going to be okay," Joshua said confidently. "I know she's going to be okay." Joshua's ebullient assurance momentarily buoyed Lisa's spirits, but she had a hard time containing her emotions.

Lisa tucked the boys into bed and then slipped into the bathroom, closed the door, melted in tears, and yet remained upbeat. The boys now knew G.G. was in prison, but they did

not know that she was living with a death penalty set to be carried out within months, and the clock was ticking. We wanted
to be honest with the boys, but we didn't need to tell them everything. Nor did we want them to be afraid. Although they had
never met their grandmother face-to-face, they had come to love
G.G. through her cards, letters, and presents to them. We really
wanted Zachary and Joshua to know their grandmother for who
she was today, not the infamous woman with the murderous
past.

The emotional ups and downs were worse than the wildest
rollercoaster ride. I knew that God had changed my life—particularly my attitude toward Mom—and the forgiveness and
freedom from resentment and bitterness that I experienced was
real. But the question I now grappled with most was, "Okay,
God. Where are you taking me? What is going to be the end of
the story?"

Lisa and I talked frequently about the new potential ramifications we faced. "We have to be okay even if your mom never
walks out of that prison," Lisa said. "We know that God has
brought you to this place, but we don't know where this story is
going to end." I agreed, but it was not an easy emotional place
to find. There were two possible scenarios we could not avoid.
One, that Mom's sentence might be carried out, and she would
be executed. Two, there was a possibility that the governor might
see a reason to commute her sentence.

And we had no clue how it would work out.

Lisa and I visited with Mom in the prison more frequently.
As part of our effort to keep doing what we always did, the boys
spent every other Friday night with Lisa's parents. Ordinarily,
Lisa and I considered that our "date night." Now, it was an
opportunity to spend time with Mother, so our date nights were
now spent in prison. At the conclusion of each visit, with the
specter of the death penalty hanging over her, Mom never said

goodbye. "See ya," she'd say with a smile. Now that we were back in contact, she refused to say goodbye. Mother knew that even if she were executed, we would see each other again in heaven, so goodbye was too final an expression.

"See ya," she said with a slight wave of her hand, as tears welled in her eyes, and the now too familiar clank of the closing prison door echoed in our ears.

CHAPTER 28

Miracles Happen

Each day was nerve wracking as we awaited news of the governor's decision on Mother's clemency request. Despite the tension that accompanied every phone call, text message, or voice mail, Lisa and I were determined to maintain a sense of normalcy for our boys throughout the summer. Once school was out and my basketball camps were concluded, we had planned to go on a family vacation to Hilton Head in early July, but we fretted that the governor might make a decision while we were away.

"Go ahead and go," Kelley advised. "We can fly you back here in an hour or two if we find out something is going to happen." The legal team thought we needed to get away from the perpetual pressure, so we discussed several contingency plans to get us back to Nashville, depending on whether the governor's announcement was good news or bad.

Armed with cell phones and beach gear, we headed off to Hilton Head and checked in to our rented condo, just a short walk from the beach. *This is going to be good,* I thought. To have some fun in the sun with the boys and Lisa and to get away from prison thoughts and the "what ifs" would be a refreshing change.

And it would have been, had I been able to stop thinking about the death penalty, prison cells, and wondering, *Is Kelley going to call me today? Have they heard anything yet? Where is the governor? When is he going to decide? What if . . .*

Certainly, I was able to relax somewhat. I got up each morning and exercised by running through the beautiful tree-lined, gorgeously manicured streets of Hilton Head, thinking and praying as I ran. Running has always been a great stress reliever for me—almost as good as Lisa's favorite methods of coping with stress: house cleaning, reorganizing, and remodeling—and besides the physical benefits, it has also been a help in maintaining my spiritual disciplines, especially my prayer life. Some of my best conversations with God have been while I've been out running in His creation. From that respect, the week at Hilton Head was great for me. Our family enjoyed the week and arrived safely back home and the governor still had not acted.

By now, Mother had been incarcerated for more than twenty-six years, most of that time waiting on the government to carry out the death penalty to which she had been sentenced. If the length of the appeals process itself is unbearable, the waiting for the governor's decision seemed interminable to me.

Gretchen returned to work from her maternity leave on July 10, surprised yet somewhat relieved that the decision hadn't come down yet. She had been worried during her maternity leave that something might happen while she was at home, and that she would not be able to be a part of it, so even after her daughter's birth on March 8, she visited Mom often and talked with her regularly by phone. She continued going to occasional meetings with the legal team, as well, to stay informed and to offer whatever assistance she could.

On July 14, Pat Williams, Mother's Bible study friend, woke up with heaviness on her heart. She had not had a doubt that Mother would walk out of prison, but this day was different. She had gone to the dentist and returned home, when suddenly, she was overcome by fear and negative thoughts. *What are you going to say to Gaile, after promising her that God would give her the desires of her heart? What are you going to do if it doesn't really happen?* Pat felt a spiritual heaviness unlike anything she had known previously in regard to Mother's case. Her mind came back to the message God had given her for Mother: "One day at a time, in the palm of My hand."

Katy, John, and George all knew the governor personally, but Phil Bredesen was not the kind of person to be influenced by those relationships. George had an especially strong, deep relationship with the governor, but even in George's meeting with Governor Bredesen, the governor did not give away his hand. He made only one commitment to George. He told him, "I will let you know what I'm going to do before I make any public announcement."

We received a call on the morning of July 14 that Governor Bredesen was holding a press conference to announce his decision. Gretchen and Kelly hurried to get from their Nashville office on 9th Avenue and Broadway to the Tennessee State Capitol building, a few blocks away. They called me on my cell phone and told me the governor would be announcing his decision in the next few minutes. I was driving the car when I received the call, and nearly drove off the road. The attorneys said they would call me back as soon as they knew anything. Gretchen and Kelly trembled as they held hands in the car on the way. This was it. Is she going to live or die?

Governor Bredesen had told George that he would let him know what he had decided before making it public and he was true to his word. About thirty minutes before ten in the morning, George Barrett's phone rang. Calling the case "complex and emotional," the governor cited the "extraordinary" sentence rendered in the case and the fact that Owens had accepted a conditional plea agreement prior to her trial. "Nearly all the similar cases have resulted in life-in-prison sentences." Bredesen advised George that he was commuting the death sentence. And she would further receive one thousand days of sentence credit— "considerably less" than she would have earned had her original sentence been life imprisonment. Gaile would therefore be eligible for parole in late spring 2012. Immediately after his call from the governor, George called Gretchen, Kelley, and John.

Joshua and I had been on our way to pick up Zachary from summer tutoring classes when I received the call. I frantically dialed Lisa at her workplace, and told her that the governor's decision was coming down in a matter of minutes. We wanted to be together when we heard the news, whether it was life or death. We quickly decided that she should head toward home, about ten minutes from where she worked, and I would continue on to get Zachary and then meet her back at the house.

Lisa left work immediately, and started toward our home. She called her mom and a couple of her closest friends along the way, informing them of the impending decision and asking them to pray.

Kelly and Gretchen didn't make it to the Capitol before they received the call from George. The attorneys nearly lost it, they were so happy! They wanted to get a message to Mother and me quickly before somebody else told either of us. They called me on one cell phone and called Mother on another, then held the cell phones up together so we could all hear each other. Between tearful sobs and garbled cell phone reception, Gretchen and Kelley told us that Governor Bredesen had commuted Mother's sentence and had even opened the possibility of parole. "We got what we wanted!" I said to Mother through the three-way call. We promised to see each other later that day. Kelley and Gretchen then went back to the office and wept tears of joy.

With tears streaming down my face, as well, I called Lisa. Practically yelling into the phone from my joy and excitement, I said, "He did it! He commuted her sentence." I could hear Lisa falling apart in a mixture of unbelievable celebration and tearful relief at the same time. I tried to explain some of the details and ramifications of the governor's decision but it was all getting splashed together in a mish mash of tears, exuberance, and trying to keep the car on the road.

A few minutes later, I pulled into our driveway at home. I got the boys out of the car and ran inside, with Lisa meeting me as soon as I burst through the door. We fell into each other's arms and embraced in one of the best hugs ever. Meanwhile, Joshua and Zachary had ambled in behind me and were just standing in the doorway, watching wide-eyed, wondering what was going on.

My phone started ringing like crazy, with people hearing the good news and wanting to congratulate us and extend their best wishes to Mother. In between the ringtones, Lisa and I gathered the boys in a group hug sort of huddle, and said, "God has answered our prayers for G.G."

Lisa and I were close to bawling but the boys' brains worked a bit differently. "Is she going to get out?" Zachary asked immediately.

"We don't know yet," I said.

"We need to keep praying about that," Lisa added, "but we sure have received good news today!"

My phone rang again and again, so I stepped outside into the warm summer sunshine to answer it, and to make some emotion-filled calls letting others know the good news. Lisa made arrangements for somebody to stay with the boys, so we could get to the prison to rejoice with Mother as soon as possible. We kept the television and radio off that day, and made sure the boys were shielded from seeing or hearing the rehashing of the case details that we knew would soon inundate the air waves.

At the Tennessee Prison for Women, an officer gave Mother a rare treat. She handed her a staff phone and said to her, "Well, who do you want to call? I know you have dozens of people you want to tell!"

"No, only one," Mom replied. She dialed the number of Pat Williams.

John Seigenthaler was on the golf course that morning when he received a phone call from a reporter associated with a Nashville television station. John wasn't sure whether the reporter was fishing for information or if he honestly wanted to get his response. "Have you heard about the case?" the reporter asked.

"No," said John. "I haven't heard a thing."

"We think the governor has acted in Gaile Owens's behalf."

"That's good news," John said with a wry smile.

John immediately called George Barrett.

"He did it, John," Barrett said matter-of-factly. "The governor commuted the sentence."

Elation washed over John; he later quipped, "It was like hitting a hole in one."

John took no credit, but instead was quick to congratulate George, who, like me, had come to the party late, long after Katy, Kelley, and Gretchen had been laboring on the case for years. But George's expertise and his influence had been effective in presenting the case for clemency and we were all deeply grateful!

That afternoon, Lisa and I coordinated our plan with Kelley and Gretchen, and headed to the Tennessee Prison for Women, where Mother was still in Unit 3, where death row inmates were housed. Kelley wrangled special permission from the warden so we could visit with Mother in nonvisitation hours, and we were grateful for the warden's approval. She wouldn't have had to let us in, but I think even the warden wanted to celebrate the governor's decision that Mother was going to live. Inmates, officers, and staff alike who had heard the news were already heaping tearful congratulations on Mother. She and I had talked by phone earlier, so she knew the governor's decision, and she had talked with Pat, as well. There was no way she could conceal her joy.

I went through the door first and even before we got into the visiting room, Mother and I seemed drawn together as though in a slow motion scene from a movie. But in reality it took only a second to sweep her into my arms and hug her in a long, lingering embrace. Tears streamed down her face and mine, mingling together. We mentally spoke a million muddled words at once, but they all sounded either like "I love you," or "Praise God." I'm not certain that any complete syllables made it out of our mouths.

Lisa, Gretchen, Katy, and Kelley followed closely behind me, and each in turn joined in hugging Mother. Mother bounced from hug to hug, saying, "I just can't believe it. This is amazing; I can't believe it!" When we moved into the visiting room and sat down, and Mother saw all of us there, with the beaming smiles on our faces and the tears trickling from our eyes, she lost it again. She had embraced each of us individually, but there was something special about seeing us all together, weeping, and laughing, and verbally replaying the events of the morning. There were repeated hugs all around, and tears of joy that flowed freely again and again when one of us caught the eye of another. We'd wipe our eyes, laugh about something, and then

someone would soon start crying all over again. But it was okay.
Mother was alive and she was going to live! It was a good day, a
really good day.

Several officers came by while we were there and they wanted
to hug and congratulate Mom, too. It was incredibly moving
and meaningful to see my mother embraced by the guards. Of
course, Mother wanted to introduce me to every one of them.
"Ooo, he's so handsome!" one of the female guards cooed. "You
got a good lookin' boy there, Miss Gaile," another said. Even in
prison, I could feel my face blushing at their compliments, but I
could tell Mother was so proud. I thanked the guards and turned
the attention back to Mother. It was, after all, her day.

We stayed for several hours before Gretchen had to leave to
care for her baby girl at home. This was one of the longest stints
she had been away from her baby since she had returned to work.
Lisa and I stayed even longer, and about the time we were ready
to leave, Pat and Gene showed up for visitation night, and the
celebration began all over again!

In granting clemency, Governor Bredesen cited two major
considerations in his decision to commute Mom's sentence:
"First, there's at least a possibility that she was in an abusive
marriage. While that in no way excuses arranging for murder,
that possibility of abuse and the psychological conditions that can
result from that abuse seems to me at least a factor affecting the
severity of the punishment.

"Second, Ms. Owens was offered a plea bargain prior to
her trial, of life imprisonment in exchange for her guilty plea.
She accepted that plea bargain, the responsibility and the
punishment, and the district attorney clearly considered that
an appropriate resolution as well." The governor pointed out
that Mother's plea bargain offer, however, was contingent on

Porterfield accepting it, as well. "When he refused, the offer was withdrawn by prosecutors and she went to trial with Porterfield as a co-defendant." It was on this basis, primarily that he granted the clemency. Governor Bredesen also noted that his office had reviewed thirty-three similar Tennessee cases of women arranging and being charged with the murder of their husbands, some involving domestic abuse and some not. He said that only two of the cases resulted in the women being sentenced to death.

"One of them, [former governor] Lamar Alexander commuted," said Governor Bredesen. "The second one I'm commuting today."

The governor could have given Mother "life in prison, without parole," which would have kept Mother alive, but in prison for the remainder of her life. But he did not.

Nor did Governor Phil Bredesen pardon Mother. He *commuted* her sentence to life in prison, and then granted her one thousand days of "good time," time taken off her sentence because of her good behavior and work within the prison. The thousand days was a statement in itself. The governor would not have done that had he not been convinced that Mother's case deserved to be commuted. No doubt, he was well aware that by doing so, he was immediately making it possible for what had been unthinkable only a few weeks ago: Mother was eligible to be paroled!

Mother's attorneys were thrilled. Convicted criminals sentenced to "life in prison" in 1985 normally were reviewed for possible parole after serving thirty years in prison. Because Mother now had a life sentence, and had served twenty-six and half years, when the governor added in the "good days," he was basically knocking off nearly three years from Mom's life sentence. Moreover, because he did not change her sentence to "life in prison without the possibility of parole," essentially, he was setting her up to be eligible for release from prison in little more than a year. While his decision did not mandate that a parole board release Mother, it did compel the board to consider her for parole at the earliest possible date. That in itself was another miracle, as far as we were concerned. A few hours ago, we didn't know whether my mother was going to live or die. Now, it was possible that Mother could be free and out playing with her grandchildren in a relatively short time!

Memories of Mother's commutation day are vivid because they were so meaningful, yet in other ways, everything seemed blurred, as though we were living in a dream. But one of the best statements from anyone in our group came from the young woman Mother looked to as her lead attorney.

As she walked down the chute to see Mother on Death Row, Gretchen thought, *I'm never going to have to do this again.*

CHAPTER 29

The Parole Hearing

I t had been more than a year since Mother's sentence had been commuted by the governor. On July 16, however, she had been allowed to live in the general population and move about like any other inmate. But she was still in prison. Then came word that Mother's first parole hearing had been scheduled.

Around eight o'clock in the morning, on September 7, 2011, Lisa and I made the trip once again to the Tennessee Prison for Women. We had no idea how many people would show up at the parole hearing. When we arrived, we were surprised to see that already a mass of people had gathered outside the prison, standing around in front of the barbed wire fences, waiting to get in to attend the hearing. Several people approached John Seigenthaler saying, "Thank you for writing those articles." There was an incredible sense of camaraderie, a feeling that we were all in this thing together.

Nevertheless, for most of the people gathered that morning, it was a novel experience to be going inside a prison. Some of them were nervous. Even the most confident person in the group felt a certain lack of control, since the prison officers were the masters of the moment, directing people regardless of status, through the security procedures. Even for Mother's supporters who had been inside a prison previously, there is something about going inside the walls of the prison that can change you. Your spirit is moved when you look into the faces of inmates. You can't help but recall that this is somebody's father, mother, son, or daughter. Worse yet, when you look into the face of the officers, you wonder, "How can you go home to a normal life after being here all day?"

Although I was nervous the morning of the parole hearing, my spirit was calm. Regardless of what happened this day, I knew now that Mother was not going to be executed. Indeed, since Governor Bredesen had been so generous in his commutation of her sentence, I felt it would be difficult for the parole board to hold her in prison for long. On the other hand, even with the commuted sentence, there were no guarantees, and the parole board was not required to release her—ever. Mother realized that, as well, especially having seen numerous other inmates go to parole hearings with high hopes of being released, only to return to their cells disappointed.

Everyone was hopeful, but aware that the board might not release Mother on the first review. The likelihood was that they would not.

I kept saying, "It doesn't make any sense that they wouldn't let her out."

"You're right, Stephen," Katy said to me. "It might not make sense to us, but the way the system works, it doesn't always release a person for parole on the first hearing." Katy had good reason to think that, having had conversations with several parole board members over recent months.

In our preparation meetings, we had discussed the various parole board members, what they might be looking for from Mother, and how they were likely to vote. Certainly, all the parole board members would want to hear expressions of Mother's remorse before they would ever consider allowing her out of prison.

The parole board review process required that for an inmate to be released on parole, at least five of the nine board members must vote for release. One board member would do the review with Mother, examining the case, and allowing character witnesses to present statements, either for or against her being released. At the conclusion of the hearing, the board member would cast the first vote. Regardless of that first vote, Yes or No, the recording of the hearing was put on DVDs and sent to the other six board members, along with the application for parole and any other necessary records. Then each parole board member would cast his or her vote electronically until four votes were received either for release or for continuation in prison. Many people have come up for parole repeatedly over the years, but have been sent back to prison again.

John had some concerns about which parole board representative would handle the initial hearing. Most likely it would be Charles Traughber of Memphis, or Patsy Bruce of Nashville. Charles Traughber was the Tennessee Board of Probation and Parole Chairman; John had written about him often over his career, and he knew Traughber to be a tough sell.

In the weeks of preparation prior to the hearing, Katy led the legal team in discussions about who should speak and in what order. The rules of the parole board mandated that the speakers bring new information or a variety of aspects to the case, rather than mere repetition of the same material by a number of speakers. If a speaker violated those rules, he or she risked being cut off.

The team decided that I should speak first, and then several people from the YWCA, Kathy Varney, friends, women who had ministered to Mother while in prison, and finally John Seigenthaler would bat clean-up, bringing hopefully the message home.

Katy, Kelley, and Gretchen prepared a large packet of materials for the parole board officers that included everything from court records to copies of the petition from "Friends of Gaile." Katy and the attorneys also visited with Mom prior to the hearing and helped prep her for the type of questions she might receive from the parole board representative. They emphasized to Mother that although it would be okay to be emotional, tears would not bring results if the officer was not convinced that Mother was sincerely remorseful.

Although Mother wanted to give herself every chance, she did not really expect to be released. Mom had seen many of her fellow inmates turned down for parole on the first review, almost as if the board didn't want to be perceived as being too lenient. In her mind, she thought, *six months will be the minimum amount of time before they might consider saying yes.* More likely, she assumed, the parole board would not release her for a year to three years.

The prison officials instructed the legal team, special guests, and those of us who would be speaking to go through security procedures first, before the others in the crowd. Ordinarily, parole hearings were held in one of the conference or meeting rooms in the prison, but because of the large number of people who wanted to attend, Mom's hearing would be held in the larger room normally used as the general population visiting area, replete with vending machines.

Lisa and I entered the room, along with John, Pat and Gene, and the attorneys. A few media people and camera operators were the only other people in the room at the time. Once the speakers and our team were settled in, the remaining spectators entered. Although I had called Brian and Aunt Carolyn informing them that the hearing was going to take place, nobody from our extended family showed up. But about ninety-three other people gathered in the visitation room along with us, for the first parole hearing.

In his seat, John looked around and was amazed at the crowd of people who had come to support Mother. The room was completely full! More chairs were required. Looking at the faces, I realized it was nothing more or less than love for my mom that had brought all these people to this room so early in the morning. As awful as it was being there, I got a good feeling.

Mother was kept in a nearby holding room, and we were told that she would not be brought in until everyone had been processed and all visitors were seated. She was permitted to meet with Gretchen briefly prior to the hearing. Gretchen tried to calm her nerves and to encourage her. "We're hoping for the best, Gaile. You deserve to get out; I believe that with all my heart, but if not, this will simply be the first of many steps."

Like the rest of us, Gretchen was elated that Mother was alive, and she had gotten her life back.

Mother's hearing was scheduled to begin at 10:00 a.m., and while our group was going through security procedures, the parole board representative, Patsy Bruce, was conducting another hearing in an adjoining room. That case had some opposition, some people who had shown up in protest of the inmate being released, so the hearing ran long. Mother's hearing would not begin until that hearing concluded and all the other people had exited the building.

Katy Varney and Kelley Henry took charge of placing each of us in the proper positions. We sat on the front row in speaking order. I sat on the end seat, with a television camera just over my shoulder. The parole board representative, Patsy Bruce, a bespectacled, blonde-haired woman I guessed to be close to Mother's age, finally entered the room and sat down at the desk across the room. She thumbed through a large notebook containing all the documents and details of Mom's case. The room grew deathly quiet. An assistant hooked up a computer and a microphone.

Ms. Bruce looked up momentarily at the crowd, and said, "Just give me a moment to get organized." Patsy Bruce's demeanor was professional but almost welcoming that day. Finally, Ms. Bruce looked at one of the officials and nodded. "Bring her in."

Wearing a light blue prison shirt, blue-jean prison pants, and white tennis shoes, with her glasses clipped over the front of her shirt, Mother walked through the door and up the side of the room, as every eye fastened upon her. I could tell that she was nervous as she made her way to the chair at the desk. Mother was seated face-to-face with Ms. Bruce, her back to the spectators. I couldn't help noticing that the desk was a few feet away from the door that led to the barbed wire chute that Lisa and I went through every time we came to the prison to visit Mother on death row.

Ms. Bruce first granted those who wished to speak on Mother's behalf an opportunity to have our say. I leaned close to Lisa and said, "Pray for me, I'm really nervous." I knew that my speaking at this hearing would be emotion-driven and, in many ways, this would be the most difficult speech of my life. Mom, too, had a hard time controlling her emotions when I stood to speak. She later said that she felt more emotion that day than she had in years.

I used no notes during my presentation, but I did have a piece of paper to which I could refer if necessary. I maintained eye contact with Patsy Bruce as much as possible. She returned my gaze steadily, looking right at me. My comments focused on the point I had made in my appeal to the governor, that as Mother's son, I was both the victim of the crime and a strong supporter of Mother's release. I asked that my mother be paroled, and that she be allowed to come home to be with her family, which now included two grandsons she had never met.

Although I expected Ms. Bruce to ask questions of me, she did not.

"Thank you very much," she said perfunctorily. She made some brief notes on her paperwork, and looked up. The women followed, each emphasizing their desire to see Mother released. Linda Knott gave a glowing character witness of Mother, and told how she had ministered in the women's prison for decades, and she had never seen anyone have a more positive influence among inmates than Mother.

Pat Williams spoke about why she and her husband Gene, who had also ministered in the prison for years, were willing to take Mother in and give her a home upon her release.

"Okay, who is the next to speak?" Ms. Bruce asked.

John rose, and said, "I'm John Seigenthaler."

Ms. Bruce responded almost lightly, "Oh, yes, we know who you are." Her comment evoked a chuckle from the spectators and broke the tension slightly. John smiled and the distinguished journalist took his position in his usual easy-going yet statesman-like manner. John did a masterful job in briefly reviewing the large number of women who had committed similar crimes, and had been released on parole within the state of Tennessee. Throughout the hearing, Ms. Bruce maintained a stern, stoic, seemingly emotionless exterior appearance, as though she wanted everyone to know that this was straightforward business. She did not flinch or respond to anything anyone said.

Then it was Mother's turn.

Ms. Bruce spoke to her politely but matter-of-factly. "You have served twenty-six years and six months on this sentence . . . I explained earlier that it is a four vote case . . . you're going to know at the end of this hearing how I vote, but that's all we will know. I've studied your case and I'm going to ask you questions that are pertinent for me before I cast my vote. Tell me, this is your opportunity in this hearing to tell me what happened."

Mother put on her glasses and read a statement she had prepared, beginning by thanking the governor for commuting her sentence, and thanking the people who had gathered to support her. She then said, "It is with immeasurable regret and remorse that I admit that I am responsible for the death of my husband, Ron Owens," the emotion filling her face and her voice almost immediately. "I ultimately put . . . was responsible for putting the wheels in motion that caused his death. I do not know that it is important to get into all the details because I bear the full responsibility.

"In December 1984, I had reached a breaking point in my marriage and did not know where to turn. As I reflect back, the difficulties experienced in my marriage had been gaining on me over the years. Divorce was not an option as I had asked for one and was told that I would never have my sons, something I could not fathom, to have my life without them. The life that I had worked so hard to achieve was being lost."

"At a point of desperation, I drove through the streets of Memphis in search of someone who would hurt my husband. He was killed on Sunday night, February 17, and my sons and I found him on the floor of our home."

"Words cannot express the remorse and regret I have from the responsibility in Ron's death. I have spent the last twenty-six years reliving that day and my actions over and over again. This will never change. I am responsible for Ron's death, and for this I am terribly sorry."

In her statement, Mother plainly stated that she is not the same woman that she was twenty-six years earlier. "None of us are promised tomorrow, but I'm asking you to allow me to have my tomorrows outside these walls with my son and my grandchildren."

John Seigenthaler shifted uneasily in his chair. John was concerned that Mom's statement was inadequate, that she had not made a good case. Mother had determined that she was not going to make any excuses, but took full responsibility for her crime. She spoke quietly, and although I was close enough to hear what she told Patsy Bruce, others in the room probably could barely hear a word she said. But Patsy Bruce heard, and she had read the record. She knew of the circumstances surrounding the crime. Her questions were right on the money, and Mother's answers seemed to be what the parole board officer wanted to hear.

In dealing with Mother, Patsy Bruce was cordial but firm. Occasionally, she clarified her questions to Mother. "Now, I only want the answer to what I am asking," she said. "I don't want anything else."

She asked Mom about the crime, walking her back through the details. Clearly, Ms. Bruce knew the answers to her questions about the crime before she even asked them, but it seemed she was more interested in Mother's personal answers. The officer was obviously looking for ownership, accountability, and remorse. She was not asking Mom to explain her actions. She was looking for an acceptance of the responsibility for the crime.

In a dramatic moment at the conclusion of the hearing, Ms. Bruce turned back to a particular page in her files. She flipped back to another page, and then returned to the page she had been viewing previously. She then repeated the process. Meanwhile the spectators sat in absolute silence.

"Just bear with me," she said quietly to Mom. "I have to be sure."

Others in the room could not see the pages in the parole officer's notebook, so we sat there with the tension mounting every time she turned back to that page. Looking at the page from across the desk, Mom recognized the page Ms. Bruce was perusing. It was the governor's commutation of her sentence.

But why was the officer examining it again? Patsy Bruce took her time, with no explanation, and no tell-tale expressions on her face.

Then, without exhibiting a crack in her professional demeanor, Ms. Bruce spoke quietly and directly across the table to Mom, "There's a lot of love for you in this room."

Ms. Bruce reminded Mother that because of the severity of the crime, her vote could easily go either way.

"I wish that it had never happened," Mom quietly told Ms. Bruce.

Patsy Bruce looked momentarily at Mom then to the rest of us, and said simply, "I have decided I am going to vote yes."

A cheer erupted in the room!

Ms. Bruce quickly added her disclaimers, that hers was only one vote, and five of nine were needed for Mom to be released on parole. That decision process could take another two to four weeks. Nevertheless, an even more enthusiastic cheer went up in the room from the spectators.

Mom could no longer contain her tears. She looked at me, and I nearly lost it as well. Ms. Bruce almost smiled as she said to Mother, "You will be on parole the rest of your life. Looking at your file and the people here today, you do not seem to have trouble making friends. Make a very good friend of your parole officer." That was special. It was clear when we walked out that Patsy Bruce was supportive of Mother being released from prison.

Patsy Bruce concluded the hearing. One of the first people to reach Mother, wrapping her in a big hug was John Seigenthaler. Then it was my turn. I hugged Mother and I thought she was never going to let go.

Afterward, we were all in a celebratory mood, and the prison officials allowed us to visit with Mom briefly in a side office. "I can't believe it," Mom repeated again and again. All too soon, it was time for us to leave. She was, after all, still in prison. During the days following the hearing, many people at the prison were pulling for Mom to get the three more needed votes. "Don't worry, Gaile," some of the prison guards encouraged her. "You'll be out of here soon."

For the next few days, every morning, Lisa checked the website of TN Board of Probation and Parole, looking to see if the votes from the other parole board members had yet been tallied. The tension mounted with every passing day that a decision had not been rendered. After a few weeks of that, we gave up looking at the screen.

Then near the end of September, early one morning, shortly before 7:00 a.m., Lisa decided to check the site while at work. When she pulled up the screen, she could hardly believe her eyes. Under the box designated as "Hearing Result" was one word after Mom's name: Parole.

Lisa used every form of communication at her disposal to contact me at work; she called, sent a text message, sent an e-mail, sent an iChat notification, anything she could, saying

"Call me!" Oddly enough, when I saw her frantic messages, it never crossed my mind that her messages had anything to do with Mother. I was afraid something was wrong. When I called Lisa back, she was so excited she could barely talk. "Get to the site," she said. "It says paroled. Your mom's been paroled!"

I pulled up the site and saw the word Lisa had seen.

Parole! I rubbed my eyes to make sure they weren't deceiving me. The parole board had decided to allow my mom out of prison after more than twenty-six years.

With Lisa still on the phone, I somehow had enough wits about me to say, "Did you call Gretchen?"

Lisa laughed. "No, I called *you!*"

"Okay, I'll call her." I made the call to Gretchen and quickly realized that she had not yet heard the news. She burst out in tears of joy. When I hung up the phone, I stepped back into my office at school and burst into tears, as well. I recalled the three times when I had similar bursts of emotion: when the execution date was set, when the governor stepped in and changed Mom's sentence, and now when she was paroled.

I asked a fellow teacher to cover my seventh grade science class for me. "Are you okay?" she asked.

"Yes, Lisa just told me that Mom's paroled," I struggled to get the words out of my mouth.

The decision came out on the morning of September 28, 2011, three weeks to the day after the parole hearing, one year to the day after Mom would have been executed, had Governor Bredesen not commuted her sentence, and oh, yes, on Gretchen and Rich's anniversary.

It was as though God was saying, "I want you to notice Who is in charge here."

I called out to the prison to try to get a message to Mother and called several other key people, especially John, and left a message for him. I didn't get a hold of Steve Wilson until I was

on the way home that day. I called Aunt Carolyn and Brian to
inform them that Mom had been paroled.

When we got home that afternoon, Lisa and I called the boys
into the den to tell them what had happened. "We have some
good news for you," I said.

Zachary's eyes brightened. "Is G.G. getting out?" he asked.

Lisa and I laughed. "Yes, G.G. got paroled and she will be
getting out of prison soon."

Like most kids, they wanted instant gratification. "When,
tomorrow?"

"No, it may take a couple of weeks for all the paperwork to
get processed," I said. "But she will definitely be getting out and
you can see her soon."

Later, Lisa, Gretchen, Kelley, and I drove out to the prison
to celebrate the good news with Mom. No longer did we have
to meet her in a private room off Death Row. Now we gathered
in the general population visiting room, the same room where
Patsy Bruce had cast the first yes vote three weeks earlier. Tears
of joy streamed down all of our faces as we embraced.

That day, I issued a brief statement through the attorneys:
"This is a beautiful day for our family. I am grateful to the
parole board for granting parole to my mother, Gaile Owens,
after twenty-six years in prison. One year ago today was the date
that Mom was to be executed had Governor Phil Bredesen not
commuted her sentence. I will always be grateful to Governor
Bredesen, to my mother's legal team, and to the thousands of
friends and strangers who have rallied behind my mom and our
family."

As always, Lisa and I tried our best to maintain our routines in the life of our family. We still were uncertain on when
Mother's processing would be complete, and when she would be

released, so we went on Zachary's previously planned weekend camping trip. While the kids were playing flashlight tag with other campers under the stars, Lisa and I went inside the tent and made a list of things we felt that we were going to have to deal with immediately. "What does she need?" we asked ourselves a zillion times. Lisa and I focused on the physical things we knew Mom would need. For instance, she had no clothing other that what Katy had purchased for Mother to wear on her release day. We knew some friends planned to give her gift cards to clothing stores, so we didn't worry too much about that.

Mom had no identification documents; she didn't have a birth certificate, social security card, or a driver's license— indispensible for life in the twenty-first century. Over the weekend, I made some phone calls to find out where we needed to start on getting Mom's identity reestablished.

She owned nothing but what she would carry out of prison, and needed everything from eating utensils to a chair to bedding to start life over again. Fortunately, Pat and Gene had invited her to come to their home. They all felt that living in their home would be a good option during her transition to life outside the prison.

I called Pat from the tent, and we talked about how we were going to handle the crowd of well-wishers who wanted to come visit Mother at Pat and Gene's home after her release from prison. We decided that it would be best to limit that number to those closest to her and the members of the legal team. Once she got settled in, she could have as many visitors that wanted to come, but we felt certain it was going to be an emotional day, and that wisdom dictated that we not overwhelm Mom with a large crowd of visitors her first day out of prison.

Sitting in the tent, talking to Pat on my cell phone, we reviewed our list of items that we thought Mother might need. I was pleasantly surprised that Pat was way ahead of me. She already had most of the immediate day-to-day needs ready for Mother.

On Friday, October 7, 2011, I took off work so I could be there when Mother walked out of prison. It was a sunny, blue-sky morning, the early fall temperatures still pleasant, short-sleeve weather. Lisa and I took the kids to school that day, then drove to the prison, arriving around 8:30 a.m. Unlike our many other visits to the prison, this time we were not permitted inside. We were to wait outside in the parking lot for Mom to be released and take the last long leg out the sidewalk and through the gate of the fence. Katy Varney was already distracting a media truck. "Just stay in the car," she instructed me, "so you don't get inundated with questions. I'll let you know when everything is ready." We gladly stayed put, with our windows tightly shut. The press did not know that I was there until I walked up behind a small group of well-wishers that had gathered in the parking lot and some television cameramen and reporters waiting with us as Mother cleared the processing inside. We didn't know where she would walk out, or what the routine was. But Deborah Johnson—the same person who had walked Mother into the prison in 1986—was the same person who walked her out in 2011.

We shuffled, joked, and laughed anxiously as we watched for her, all of us peering intently through the cyclone fence, with stacks of razor wire at its base and all around the top. Then suddenly, there she was! It was an awkward but wonderful moment when we saw her coming out of the prison complex, accompanied by a tall female prison officer on her right, and Warden Johnson, on her left, walking slightly behind her. Mother pushed a yellow laundry cart containing all her earthly possessions.

Unfortunately, the new blouse Katy had bought for her didn't fit, so Mom wore a gray prison sweatshirt, black pants, and black shoes, and her face was radiant. In her left hand, she clutched a sealed envelope, her release papers I guessed. She was smiling nervously and shedding tears of joy at the same time as she stepped past the razor-wire fence and into a new life of freedom. The moment people saw her come out of the building, they started cheering and applauding, calling out words of encouragement. Mom let loose of her cart and came directly to me. I was waiting for her with open arms, and hugged her for a long time, feeling her convulsing in tears in my embrace.

"We love you, Gaile!" some people called out to her.

Then everybody was hugging Mom, including Linda Oakley, one of her former cellmates who had returned just so she could be with Mother when she was released. It was a highly emotional moment. Mom was fifty-eight years of age, she had been in prison on death row for more than twenty-six years, she had come within three months of being executed, and now she was starting life all over.

Mom did not want to speak to the media, so Pat and Gene pulled their car up close to where Mom was standing. Gene popped the trunk and took Mom's few possessions from the cart and placed them inside. "We need to get you out of here, Mom," I said, guiding her away from the crowd. Gretchen, Mom, and Linda Oakley got into the car with Pat and Gene. Mom dabbed the tears from her eyes with a handkerchief someone gave her. She turned and waved out the back window as Gene pulled out of the parking lot in his silver Honda with the Tennessee license plate bearing the never more poignant slogan, "Choose Life."

I waited till they were gone, then turned around to address the media. I read a brief statement that Katy had helped me to prepare and Lisa and I had tweaked, expressing our joy at Mom's release and thanking her many supporters and also answered a couple of questions. After a few minutes, Katy Varney swept in and thanked the media for coming, and we were on our way.

I had remained focused and stoic through most of the emotionally moving scenes surrounding Mom's release, but when Lisa and I finally got in our car, I leaned my head on the steering wheel, and just sat there for several minutes with tears filling my eyes. Lisa wrapped her arms around my shoulders and her hand around my head as she hugged me and we cried together. It was over, finally over.

Lisa and I stopped by a sandwich shop on the way out to Gene and Pat's home. We had invited a very small group of friends, including Gretchen and her husband Rich, John Seigenthaler and Bob Starnes, and Katy Varney and they got there before Lisa and I did. Kelley was out of town working on another case.

To our delight and surprise, when we arrived, Mother opened the door and welcomed us to her new home.

It was a festive, joyful time of celebration at Pat and Gene's comfortable home, with lots of laughter and photographs. We were all so grateful for what God had done, and how He had used each person in the group in some special way in Mother's life. Pat showed Mom around the house, and took her upstairs to see her new bedroom. Some people had sent along some gifts for Mother, and we all enjoyed watching her open her presents.

The welcoming committee didn't overstay their welcome, and before long, it was just Pat and Gene, Lisa and me, and the woman who now was known by a name rather than a number. When all the well-wishers had said "See ya later," Lisa and I sat around the table with Mom.

Prior to our arrival, she had changed out of her prison sweat-shirt and into a decorative "Arizona" T-shirt that Pat had given to her. It was wonderful to sit down with Mother with no time limits, in a room without locks, and in a place not surrounded by razor wire. The dramatic rollercoaster ride on which we had been careening and jolting along for so long had come to an abrupt stop. Everything felt so . . . so normal! And it felt good. We all knew there would be some uncomfortable bumps in the road during Mother's transition, but for now, we basked in what so many families take for granted—simply the opportunity to be together. We talked and laughed, and nibbled at the food on the table. After a while, Lisa fell asleep on Pat and Gene's couch. Like me, she was emotionally and physically exhausted.

Mother, too, slept soundly that first night. She knew that Pat and Gene genuinely loved her and she was in a safe place.

The next day, we brought Zachary and Joshua to meet their grandmother for the first time. It was astonishing how natural they were with her, and she was with them. "Hey, G.G.!" they called out to her, hugging her right away and talking non-stop. Gretchen's husband, Rich, is a professional photographer, and he had helped us prepare some special family photographs for Mother, which Lisa had framed and we had the boys present to her. Mother was overjoyed. Zachary's class members at school had all made cards for Mom, with Bible verses and handwritten messages, and he gave those to her. She tried not to fall apart, and simply enjoy everything, but she didn't always succeed.

G.G. showed the boys the garden and the boys soon had G.G. out in the yard, kicking a ball. One of her prison dreams had been to walk in a park with her grandchildren. Now, here she was doing it.

As I watched, it struck me that God had brought things full circle. Once again, He confirmed to me that I had done what He had asked me to do. It was as though He was speaking to my heart and saying, "Stephen, this is the real fruit of your labor . . . and there will be much more."

On Monday, we went downtown and met with the parole officer to whom Mom would be accountable; we found the office of her social worker, went and got Mom's identification card and her medicine, and then the following day, we did more everyday life chores, setting Mom up with all that she would need to function.

Most of what Mom needed, Pat and Gene already had gathered for her. The gracious, loving couple made everything in their home available to Mom. They put no constraints on her, and no time-table on her stay; they simply opened their hearts and their home and said, "You are welcome here."

Mom didn't go to church that first weekend, but since then, Mom has been in church nearly every week. The first Sunday she attended services outside prison, she went with Pat and Gene to their church.

The pastor didn't embarrass Mom or call attention to her being in church that first Sunday, but after the service, a number of people made it a point to welcome her. Mom was home.

CHAPTER 30

Back to the Future

I magine living in confinement on another planet for twenty-
six years, with little communication with the world you once
knew on earth, and then suddenly after more than a quarter of
a century, you are dropped abruptly back into a society that has
progressed at an exponential pace. The enormity of the transition Mother faced as she stepped outside the walls of the Tennessee Prison for Women was equally overwhelming.

As our family began a new part of the journey with Mom,
Lisa and I often joked, "Okay, forgiveness and reconciliation—
now what?" We recognized that we were not in heaven yet, and
none of us were perfect people, not Mom, or us, so we understood that forgiveness and reconciliation were going to be an
on-going process for all of us.

I knew that having a relationship with G.G. would have a
profound impact on Zachary and Joshua, as well as Lisa and
me. I was thrilled that our children would have the opportunity
to know their grandmother. Yet, with all the excitement of the

process, there was a bit of a burden, too, as I contemplated how Mom's release would impact my relationships with my other family members, especially Brian and Aunt Carolyn.

Aunt Carolyn had been so good to Brian and me over the years. We hadn't seen eye to eye on everything, and I had wished that she had been more supportive of Mother's release, but we have all chosen a different path to walk over the years. I have loved her all my life, and that wasn't going to change, especially now that Mother was free.

I assumed Aunt Carolyn would not make a trip to Nashville to see Mother, but I hoped an opportunity might arise in which I could take Mother to visit her. Brian seemed unsettled by Mother's release, as though she was going to pop up out of nowhere in his life. I assured Brian that Mom was not going to show up unexpectedly on his doorstep.

What was life going to look like for Lisa and our children and me?

What is our relationship with our family members? How can we lessen the tension with Brian and Aunt Carolyn? We had a lot of questions. Mom realized that she may have to go to her grave and never have a restored relationship with both of her sons, but her prayer continues that our family will one day be reunited.

The Christian community that had rallied around Mother throughout the clemency run continued to minister to her in tangible ways upon her release from prison. Sometimes in the frenzy and flurry of the publicity, under the glare of the television camera lights, people are quick to offer their support, but when the crowds dissipate and the cameras go away, oftentimes many of the well-wishers and do-gooders disappear, as well.

Not so with the people who had supported Mother, some of whom had supported her long before I ever did. People went above and beyond our greatest expectations in helping my mother put her life back together once outside prison. People bought her clothes, gift cards, and even raised money to help her purchase a used car with only twenty thousand miles on it. Pat helped Mother get reacquainted with driving a car. The speed of modern traffic was a bit frightening to her at first, but she adapted easily.

When Mother first came out of prison, she met with her parole officer who assigned a social worker, a counselor who helped Mother make the transition to life on the "outside." But we also wanted Mother to meet with counselors at The Next Door, a biblically based counseling center that helps women who are re-entering society from incarceration, rehabilitation, or homelessness (www. http://www.thenextdoor.org). Although Mom was well adjusted within the prison, I felt strongly that she would need counsel in dealing with everything from making choices in a restaurant, to how she would respond when people recognized her as a convicted criminal. There was also the possibility that Mom may have to deal with a new kind of guilt—guilt that she was free while others whom she knew personally were still incarcerated. The Next Door had offered its professional services to Mother free of charge, so I was glad when Mother accepted their offer.

She had been receiving six different medicines in prison, which the prison doctors prescribed and the prison had provided. Now that she was out, she was responsible for her own medications, but she had no money, no job, and no insurance. The volunteer doctors and nurses at Siloam Family Health Center (http://www.siloamhealth.org) where Gretchen's sister works examined Mother at a reduce rate, assisting her in extricating herself from any unnecessary medications, and helping her secure the medicines Mom required at minimal cost.

When we found out that Mother was going to be released from prison, we put out feelers to friends asking if anyone knew of a job that might be suitable for Mother during the transition period. Clearly, after being in prison for two and a half decades, her skill set was somewhat limited and there were many jobs for which she was not qualified. But for her own sense of self worth, not to mention her own financial stability, Mother needed to work. Friends helped Mother get a job at Thistle Farms, a social enterprise recovery program operated by the women of "Magdalene," a ministry to women, in which the women can gain needed job skills, learn responsibility and cooperation, while creating many natural, handmade body care products (http://www.thistlefarms.org). The products are sold in more than two hundred retail outlets and the proceeds are plowed back into the organization to help other women rebuild their broken lives.

Mom started out working three days a week and did so well, by early December she was promoted to a full time position—which included insurance benefits. When her parole officer granted permission for Mother to travel out of the state, Mother's role at Thistle Farms expanded, allowing her to visit other states to represent the products. Mom was truly making great strides in her transition, and we were all so proud of her.

A dentist in the area offered Mother free dental work upon her release. This was a sizable donation since Mom's dental care for the past quarter of a century had been minimal to nothing, and she had several serious dental problems.

The transition has not been without its occasional points of tension though.

When Mother first got out of prison, we were together a lot. Little by little, I had to wean her from dependence on me. I knew it was important that she take responsibility for herself, plus she had Gene and Pat to help her with the daily decisions and acclimating to life in the twenty-first century. Simple things that we take for granted—e-mail, phone text messaging, as well as airport security, and so much more—did not even exist when Mother went behind the prison walls in 1986. It was an entirely new world to which she was adjusting.

Lisa and I added a cell phone to our account for Mother's use so she could keep in touch with us. Not surprisingly, during the early months of the transition, once Mother learned the basics of the phone, her calls, e-mails, and text messages to me became incessant. At first, every time I heard the tone on my cell phone and saw that the contact was from Mother, I tried to respond to her immediately. Most of the messages were about minor issues, or similar to those made by a teenager who had just discovered a whole new world of communication opportunities. But I was in the midst of teaching and coaching, and raising two young boys. My life was busy. So although I was delighted to help Mother, we did have to set some healthy boundaries on how often we needed to be in contact with each other.

Overall, though, the transition period has gone amazingly smooth. Mother's and my post prison relationship continues to build on a firm foundation. At times, I've spoken quite bluntly with her, "Mother, God has given you a second chance. What you do with that opportunity is up to you."

Of course, she knows that, and I recognize that her new life is in God's hands, not mine. Mother has to depend on Him now that she is out of prison, just as much as she did when she was languishing in isolation on death row.

After a few months, Mother began talking about the possibility of going to Memphis to see her ailing older brother Wilson. I knew what that might entail. "Mother, I don't think we are ready for that yet," I told her honestly.

Then Wilson's conditioned worsened.

Aunt Carolyn called and to my dismay informed me, "The doctors say Wilson may not live much longer, maybe not more than another day, possibly as little as five or six hours, and I'm not sure I could live with myself if he died without Gaile having the opportunity to see him."

To my surprise, I heard myself saying that I would bring Mother to Memphis to visit Wilson at the hospital.

Mother arranged to take off a day of work, so we could drive to Memphis and see Wilson. I awakened around 5:00 a.m. with anxious thoughts of what this day might bring. I e-mailed friends, informing them that for some reason, I was nervous and I needed some extra prayer support. I turned my mind to the Scripture, and the first verse that came to mind was from Deuteronomy, reminding me that God would go before me.

Why are you anxious, I asked myself. *The Lord knows what's going to happen in Memphis today.* As I focused on the Scripture and that thought, my anxiety disappeared and I felt at ease.

I picked up Mother and we drove to Memphis. I noticed Mother stiffen as we passed by the first road sign declaring, "Welcome to Memphis." Other than one appeal hearing, this was the first time Mother had seen Memphis in more than two decades. Passing by the tree-lined neighborhoods as we made our way to the hospital, I could see her blinking back tears.

We walked into the hospital to see Mom's brother, Wilson, who had suffered with cerebral palsy all his life, and was now very ill. Wilson had beaten the odds several times before, but his health had deteriorated to the place where he could no longer function without assistance. The doctors were giving him no hope.

Wilson recognized Mother immediately when we entered the hospital room. It was the first time he'd seen his sister in more than twenty-seven years, and he cried when he saw her. Mother and Aunt Carolyn saw each other around Wilson's bed and for the first time in years, spoke directly to each other face-to-face. Mom asked questions about Wilson's condition and the doctors' prognosis, and Aunt Carolyn answered her questions openly.

The visit concluded and after a while, Mother, Aunt Carolyn, and I all walked out together. Mother was very emotional. She looked at Aunt Carolyn and said, "I can't tell you how much this means to me, that you would allow me to come see Wilson."

"Well, you're welcome," Aunt Carolyn replied.

Mother then looked directly into Aunt Carolyn's eyes and said softly, "I love you."

"I love you, too," Aunt Carolyn said.

The two sisters hugged.

"Wilson asked me if I was coming back."

"He says that to everybody," said Aunt Carolyn. "We'll just have to see what the future brings."

I was barely out of Memphis on the way back to Nashville, when my phone rang. Aunt Carolyn wanted to know how I felt that the visit had gone. I told her that I thought it had gone as well as could be expected.

Mother was contemplative on the way home. She didn't realize what that visit would stir up within her. Just seeing the sign, "Welcome to Memphis," brought with it enormous emotional baggage. During the drive, Mother looked at me and said "You've given me the best day I've had since I've been out of prison. First, I have been able to spend the whole day with you, and then to go see Wilson and Carolyn, and to have that go well."

How ironic that God would use Wilson to bring the two sisters together after nearly thirty years.[1] I was emotionally drained, but I smiled.

CHAPTER 31

Free Indeed

In March 2012, about six months after Mother had been released, she went along with Lisa to watch the high school basketball team I helped coach win the state basketball championship. As she sat in the arena grandstands, with all the excitement of the game, Lisa noticed that Mother was quiet and reserved. Mom later e-mailed us and said, "I realize now all the things that Ron missed."

Perhaps for the first time, even more than the impending threat of a death sentence, that event brought home to Mother the enormity and the endless ramifications of her decisions and the actions she took nearly three decades earlier. Seeing me out on the basketball court, doing what I loved, coaching a bunch of young men to be and give their best—just like Dad used to do—forced Mother to recognize what Dad missed, what she had missed, and yes, what I was never able to experience because of her choices.

Dad never coached a state championship team, but he did coach Brian and me, teaching us how to overcome obstacles and keep pressing onward toward the goal. Mother's actions deprived him of the opportunity to be in the stands that night, cheering on our team, exulting in the accomplishments of his son. Her actions ripped from me the potential thrill of turning around, waving and smiling at my father after the buzzer sounded, watching together as our team members leaped into each others' arms, hoisting some of the stars of the game onto their shoulders, seeing the look on Dad's face as his son's efforts paid off in the lives of the next generation. It was merely a basketball game—a big game, to be sure—but what it symbolized to Mother and to me was a lifetime of missed opportunities.

In truth, we all missed a lot that we can never get back. But today is a new day, and we can choose to make the most of the opportunities God gives to us. That is part of the ongoing process of being set free.

Who needs to be set free?

Mother did. I did. Perhaps you do, as well.

The son or daughter who has held onto anger against a parent; the marriage partner whose trust was betrayed; the parent whose child has forsaken his or her upbringing and has lived contrary to the values the parent believes; the friend who has been offended; the business partner who suffered financial setbacks because of someone else; the dedicated worker who has been terminated unfairly; the list could go on and on.

Who needs to be set free? Anyone who has ever been wounded or hurt by the words, actions, or attitudes of someone else.

While most people will never experience the horror of violent crime among their family members, everyone has pain from the past, wrongs inflicted upon them, times when they have been mistreated physically, emotionally, or spiritually. The only remedy for those wounds is forgiveness. True freedom can only be found through reconciliation between people who have long been at war, physically, emotionally, or spiritually. As much as I appreciate social programs, rehabilitation programs, and every group that is helping people to deal with the pain they have experienced at the hands of other people, I believe that the words of Jesus are more relevant for us today than ever. The Great Physician said, "The truth shall set you free . . . and if I set you free, you will be free indeed" (John 8:32, 36, author paraphrase).

Before I went to see Mom in prison, I thought that I had released a lot of my anger and bitterness. But I didn't realize what a heavy burden I had been carrying all those years. What I discovered as Lisa and I walked out of that prison after that first visit with my mom was that I had been carrying a much heavier load than I thought, some of which I was not even aware because I was so wrapped up in trying to make it through each day and night.

But of this I am sure: The years *since* that afternoon in 2009, when Mother and I first sat face-to-face and extended forgiveness and began the process of reconciliation in our relationship, have been the best years of my life so far! I have been set free, and am no longer encumbered by the invisible load I once lugged around with me. The freedom I have known since that burden of hatred, resentment, and bitterness has been lifted off my shoulders is beyond comprehension. Finding forgiveness myself, and extending forgiveness to my mother—and to others—has set me free. Living without a conflicted heart has been absolutely liberating. Indeed, God has given me a peace that passes understanding.

Some people may wonder: "Is it really possible that such a seriously damaged relationship can be reconciled?"

Yes, it is! Mother and I are living proof that such reconciliation is possible. Unfortunately, many people want to be reconciled without first dealing with forgiveness. If you reconcile without forgiveness, you are just asking for trouble. It won't work. You are simply giving the enemy another opportunity to disillusion you.

Society says you can be cordial and reconcile without messing with that sticky forgiveness issue. "Just be nice." "Can't we all just get along?" Unfortunately, we can't. And if you buy into that idea rather than dealing with repentance—turning away from sin and wrong—and forgiveness, you are setting yourself up for more disappointment.

But why do I have to forgive? You may be wondering.

I've had people ask me, "Stephen, why did *you* have to forgive? You were the victim, not the perpetrator."

My answer is simple: You can only carry a burden for so long. I carried a huge burden for more than twenty years. Though some people may say, "You had a right to carry a grudge," I don't see it that way.

More importantly, Jesus doesn't look at resentment and anger, jealousy, malice, or bitterness that way. To Him, the issue is not the size or the scope of the sin, not the horror, magnitude, means, or the audacity of the crime. All sin is deadly, and all sinners are living on a spiritual Death Row. The question is "Have I ever sinned?" and the answer is yes. If I've ever sinned, I need the forgiveness that only comes from God.

Jesus told a story of a person who owed an amount tantamount to ten million dollars in today's currency. When the person was forgiven that huge amount, he went out and found someone who owed him a paltry twenty bucks. "Give me what you owe me, or I'm going to have you tossed into prison!" he railed.

When the gracious person—who incidentally was the king of the land—heard that the person whom he had forgiven the ten million was treating the person who owed the twenty so offensively, the king said to him, "I forgave you that debt because you asked me. Shouldn't you have had mercy on the person who owed you, just as I had mercy on you?" Angry, the king threw the calloused, merciless person into the prison and said, "You will stay in here until you pay back what you owe!" Which of course, he couldn't.

Then Jesus added a powerful statement: He said, "So My heavenly Father will also do to you if each of you does not forgive his brother from his heart" (Matt. 18:35). Clearly, Jesus takes this matter of forgiving rather seriously. If I am going to follow Him, I can do no less.

Jesus also says if we won't forgive others the wrongs they have done against us, His heavenly Father will not forgive us (Matt. 6:14–15). That is a sobering fact.

For years, I knew what forgiveness meant but chose to limit my expression of it. But the turning point in my life came when I realized God was showing me, "What you are receiving so freely from Me and from others, you must extend to your mother." So often, we're okay when we are on the receiving end of forgiveness. But God expects forgiveness to go both ways. He wants us to seek forgiveness for what we have said, done, and thought, for how we have hurt Him and others, but then He also wants us to extend His love and forgiveness to others.

At some point, I realized that I had no choice whether to forgive Mother, regardless of what she had done. I had to forgive her, because God had forgiven me. And I desperately needed—and continually need—His forgiveness.

Carrying that anger, malice, or any other burden can be the cause of your own demise, physically, emotionally, and especially spiritually. Prior to forgiving Mother, even at my best moments,

I could not shake the ghosts that haunted me with my own permission. Oh, sure; I could put on a "happy face." But in my alone times, I knew the burden was still there.

Only when you have been willing to let God do "spiritual surgery" in your life, allowing Him to remove the cancer of sin and replace it with His unconditional love, can you ever know the wonderful changes that He can bring about in you. If you choose to live in denial, you will not alleviate the pain. Quite the opposite, the pain gets worse and the burden gets heavier. On the other hand, if you choose to forgive, you can live in freedom.

Forgiveness is not merely an isolated action; it is a continuous attitude. It is an ongoing choice, a daily—indeed, moment by moment—decision of your will. You will still struggle at times, and have obstacles to overcome; there can be no victory if there are no challenges. But there is tremendous relief when you know your conscience is clean, when you have forgiven others and you know you are forgiven by God, by other people, and you have genuinely forgiven yourself.

Certainly, while we all need to forgive the people who have hurt us, not everyone who forgives has to go on and reestablish the relationship. I chose to be reconciled with my mother, and she with me, but the forgiveness does not depend on the reconciliation. For instance a child who was abused by a parent must forgive that parent, but that does not mean he or she has to have a relationship with that person.

For me, that meant, although I had forgiven Sidney Porterfield for bludgeoning my father to death, I did not have the type of relationship with him that mandated I be a part of his life. But I can honestly say, I have forgiven him. I hold no rancor in my heart toward the man who played such a significant role in my life without even knowing me.

And that's part of the good news, too. In true forgiveness, the past offenses no longer rule you. Of course I still remember what happened to my father and how it happened. But I am free of it. Not because I don't think of it, but it no longer controls me.

One of the best things forgiveness did for me was it gave me an ability to look my kids in the eyes and tell them honestly that I did what I believed God wanted me to do. I didn't always feel like forgiving. I didn't always desire reconciliation. But with God's help, I continued to take the next step of obedience into the unknown, trusting Him to bring good out of what the devil meant for evil. And He has.

Forgiveness is not always easy. Some people want to give the impression that for those of us who trust in Jesus Christ, forgiveness and reconciliation are natural. Maybe that's true for some people, but that has not been so for me.

Holocaust survivor Corrie ten Boom once said, "Forgiveness is to set a prisoner free, and to realize the prisoner was *you*." I would concur.

What I've come to realize is that Gaile Owens was not the only member of our family imprisoned for more than a quarter of a century. I was equally as bound and shackled by my bitterness, anger, and the broken trust that decimated my life that night in 1985 when I found my dying father. The seething resentment I felt toward my mother for all those years continued to smolder, like hot lava beneath the surface of a volcano, and could have destroyed my life had I not been willing to forgive. Had I ignored forgiveness, either for my mother or myself, I would have continued to go through life dragging a ball and chain. But I thank God every day that my mother has been set free, from prison and from the past. And I thank God that I have been set free, as well.

If you will trust God and do what He tells you to do, you can muster the courage to forgive those who have hurt you so severely, to be reconciled with those for whom reconciliation is possible, and you will discover for yourself what it truly means to be *Set Free!*